On the Other Side
Love...Sex...Marriage

Sex, God's Way
Part II

BY WES MULLINGS, D.D.

The contents of this work, including, but not limited to, the accuracy of events, people, and places depicted; opinions expressed; permission to use previously published materials included; and any advice given or actions advocated are solely the responsibility of the author, who assumes all liability for said work and indemnifies the publisher against any claims stemming from publication of the work.

Dorrance Publishing Co
585 Alpha Drive
Pittsburgh, PA 15238
Visit our website at *www.dorrancebookstore.com*

ISBN: 978-1-6366-1369-7
eISBN: 978-1-6366-1946-0

CONTENTS

Chapter

PREFACE II

It has now been 50 years, a half-century and 5 degrees since the first publication of *On the Other Side - Love...Sex... Marriage* (Vantage Press, 1970). So much of the world has changed. Back then it was a time in America that Women's Liberation, Feminist Theology, Black Theology and racial inequality was front-page news week after week after week. These were early years in exercising my passion for preaching the Gospel. My primary concern for writing the book then was to reach the Black community in the area of family and individual guidance in relationships. I wasn't aware of any minority clergy addressing those problems at the time and so I began to write. I was told that "Black" folks didn't like to read. So I made it a point of keeping it short.

I was experiencing the most traumatic period of my life at that time: a divorce. It was my hope that I could help others to avoid not only my mistakes but the lessons I had learned from the hundreds of counselees I had interacted with as a chaplains assistant in the U.S. Army. At that most traumatic time in my life, I reached out to Tom Skinner to intercede on my behalf. She agreed to meet with him during divorce proceeding she initiated, Tom came back to me with devastating news. She had given me an ultimatum that I had to stop preaching the Gospel if I wanted her to come home. To me, this was not an option!!! In fact, this accelerated my fervor for preaching. I accepted more preaching invitations and even received several for radio broadcasts. My consolation rested in I Cor. 7:15: “But if the unbelieving depart let them depart. A brother or a sister is not under bondage is such cases; but God has called us to peace.”

Many years later after completing undergrad and grad schools, I founded Christian Dating Service Int’l (1980-2004). The concept was to build Christian families worldwide by introducing Christian singles of the same and similar faiths to each other. Within a year we were reaching millions of viewers and listeners with our commercials, with over 200 radio and TV stations in major and minor markets. This resulted in tens of thousands of Christian singles I had the honor of serving in those 24 years. Words cannot express how much I enjoyed using my counseling training to advance the health and happiness of our membership. See Chapter I. No, you won’t be able to Google me, I was mandated to remain in the background as coordinator (versus chairman and founder). During this time I also engaged a private counseling practice for a few years.

Looking back, I realize that only 12% of the membership was African-American. So my focus now in writing this sequel in 2020 is the whole body of Christ in this Part II addition (original manuscript included).

I believe it was God’s providence to slow down the process of this books release to allow my input on the 2020 election.

What lessons can **all** of Christianity and Christian leadership learn from this election??? For answers , let's consult our ultimate authority. II Timothy 2:4 - "*No man that warreth entangleth himself with the affairs of this life; that he may please Him who hath chosen him to be a soldier.*" Every Christian knows that in this life we are in a war.

Some years ago, while I was meeting with Johnnie Cochran on a potential law suit among other things. He used a term in his analogy of my case, I have never heard an attorney use. He responded to me, "Wes, that situation is too "tentacled," I wouldn't be able to handle it at this time." I kind of sensed he was putting a lot of time in building a franchise and establishing a brand. I can count on one hand the people I have met with his level of charisma, charm, humor and wit.

I've never been political. But I perceive politics as being "tentacled." This would obviously lead to entanglement. God is speaking here and making it quite clear that no one who takes up the mantle of spiritual leadership should indulge politics. However, like all rules, there are exceptions to every rule, such as Martin Luther King Jr., etc., etc., etc. With the same mind set, when rendering to Caesar (Mark 12:17"...render to Caesar the things that are Caesars, and to God the things that are God's."); voting is a sacred yet *private* matter between the individual and his/her God. No Church, individual or institution has the right to violate this privacy.

God, in His eternal wisdom recognized this entanglement would only bring about **division** (even in the Church), a major tool of Satan, ruler and god of this world (II Cor. 4:4). He is a master strategist. Hopefully Christianity will learn a lesson here.

The Christian lives in 2 worlds. One – This present evil world (Gal. 1:4) and two – The Kingdom of God, here and now (Lu. 17:21) as well as future. While there is separation of Church and State, patriotism is spelled out and encouraged throughout Scripture.

The greatest patriotic film I have witnessed is "Sargent York," played by Gary Cooper in 1941. A WWI film that every true American should view (available on YouTube). This beautiful once upon a time in America film, reflecting patriotism, honor, integrity and selflessness should be required viewing for every aspiring politician as well as existing politicians. It's a moment of personal pride for me to know that I spent most of my military time in this famous 82nd division. Shame on Encyclopedia Britannica for omitting this amazing war hero & icon from their biography list. Their board of directors should be confronted.

PREFACE

To many Christians, the word "sex" relates to thoughts that spell tabooed and hidden feelings of inner suspicion which come to the surface as shyness and sometimes guilt. As young people growing up, we are sometimes guilty. As young people growing up, we are sometimes expected to sit on our sexual feelings and act as if they don't exist. Because of this erroneous approach, many avenues of knowledge, martial success and male-female relationships have been disastrously distorted and torn asunder.

The author's purpose in writing this book is to go through the dating stage beyond the closed doors of the married couple. Here is where we'll find the deep secrets and inner frustrations that can permanently impair the foundation of a good marriage. Here is where we can examine those necessary ingredients to be found in the development of a warm and happy marriage, as was designed by our Creator.

My experience in reading Christian materials on this subject has led me to no practical applications and/or conclusions in certain vague areas. We have been guilty of producing the "extremes" (answers) void of the "means" (observable and practical ways of getting to the answers). It is my desire to clarify the "means" in many of these generalized areas, thereby making what

I say as easy as possible to be read and understood by the young, as well as older adults. I believe that part of this vagueness can be attributed to the communication patterns utilized by a white middle-class echelon who scratch the issues rather than exploit the depths for the sake of protocol and traditional, fundamental "couthness." This has impaired, to great extent, the understanding and clarity on issues both relevant and essential for therapy in these hushed areas.

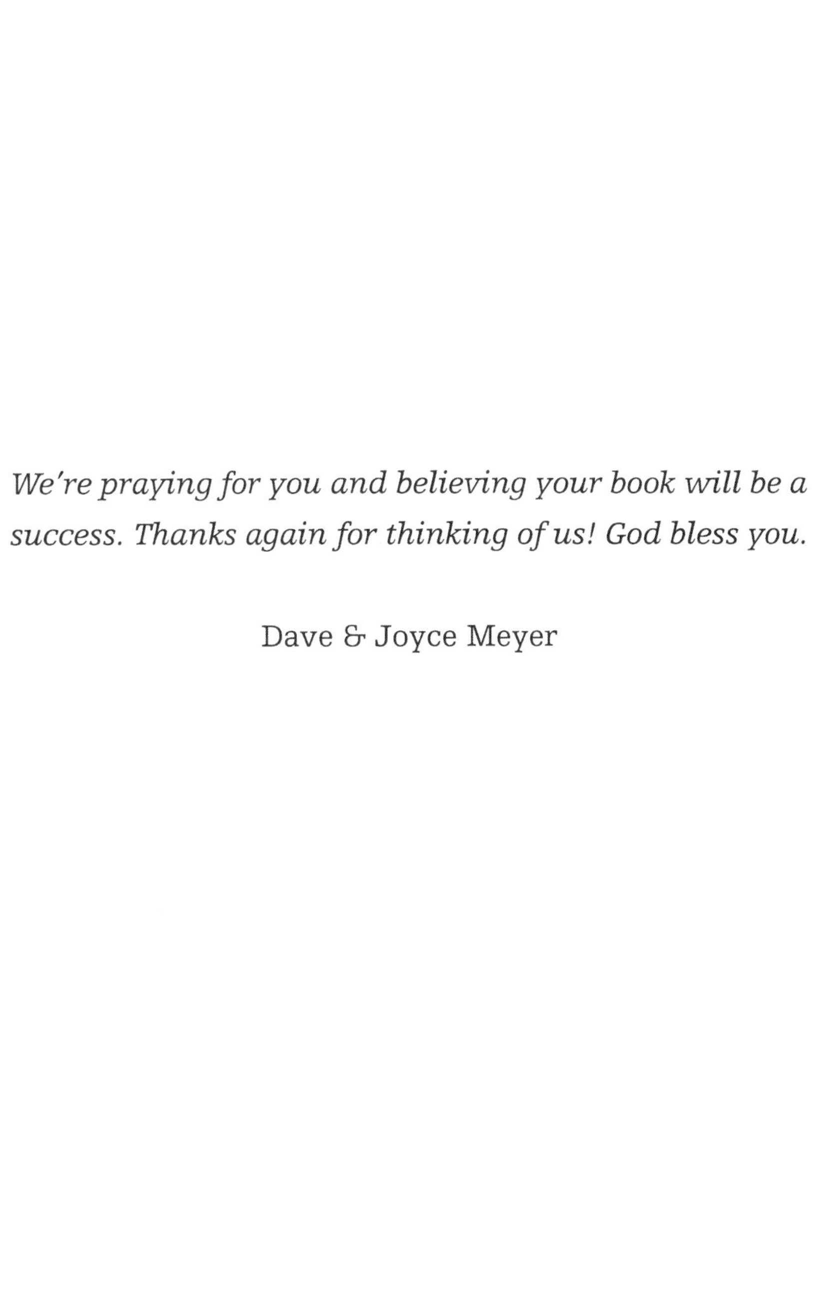

We're praying for you and believing your book will be a success. Thanks again for thinking of us! God bless you.

Dave & Joyce Meyer

Endorsements

On the Other Side is a provocative and sensitive approach to love, sex and marriage with high moral values and deep spiritual implications

Sandy F. Ray, Pres., Empire Baptist Missionary Convention; V.P. National Baptist Convention

Long overdue has been an honest discussion about sex in marriage from a Biblical perspective. Further overdue has been a Biblical perspective written by a Black Man. *On the Other Side* is a must.

Tom Skinner

I would highly recommend the book to the clergy as well as to young couples considering marriage and those already married.

Joseph Daniels, M.D., Neuro-Psychiatrist, Ass't. Clinical Prof., N.J. College of Medicine and Dentistry

Comprehensive. Extraordinary. Holistic. This is must reading for every Christian in this generation; and a challenge for the curious non-christian.

--Archbishop Angelo M. Rosario

As both a practicing Christian and educator I experience "On The Other Side" as historic, extraordinary & prophetic. I've known the author over 40 years and have witnessed first hand his caring and empathetic compassion on the subject matter. I highly recommend this book for Christians and non-Christians alike.

--Dr. Erma Percival

DISCOVERY

During my Army tour of duty as a Chaplain's assistant, I encountered problems of married couples to be able to write another book. Many of those experiences were very tragic. As a results of this experience alone, I have concluded that, of all the interpersonal relationships individuals will try to successfully construct, marriage is truly the hardest. I have listened to the stories of many women who, by being under the influence of frustration, depression or just plain feelings of loneliness, had embarked on careers in extramarital affairs. The ironical thing to me is that many of these women were both loved and sexually satisfied by their husbands. But somewhere along the line after their indulgence, they met someone that satisfied their sexual needs a little better. Then, as usual, one disaster led to another. As the saying goes, "He who travels the wrong road makes the journey twice." Once one has embarked on the trail of the extramarital affair, the initial marriage-life will never be the same. The continual anxiety to meet with that one, experiencing the new-found excitement in a new body-communion, etc., always directs your full-fledged attention away from your spouse. Personally, I feel this is a worse dilemma (living this dual life) than a divorce. When two people cannot build a relationship that pledges total allegiance and reliance on one another in everything—despite the weather conditions, depressions, etc.—they have failed. And whether or not they openly admit this to each other, the oil will come to the surface of the water, even if it takes 25 years for these hidden feelings to make themselves known. In most cases, at this point, it's too late.

Many Christians might perhaps crucify me for mentioning some of these things. However, I feel led to bring up the thoughts that sometimes lie latent in our inner being. One of our troubles is that we don't like to be honest with one another in admitting our weaknesses. Discussing the filth that can enter into our minds and thoughts! And would you believe that none of us is invulnerable? Some Christians carry on with such a superfluous attitude of piety that one looking on might very well become disheartened from seeking advice, thinking that he or she alone is hit with lustful thoughts let's face facts. God didn't make any of us perfect. However, as children of God, there is more power and grace available to us to counter such thoughts. At the point of entry of these lustful thoughts, they should be taken care of right then and there.

The Psalmist used the Word of God as his refuge in keeping clean and untouched by the claws of sin: "Thy Word have I hid in my heart that I might not sin against thee." His therapy was to become so occupied with what God had to say to him though his written word, that there wasn't enough room for anything else. The practical application for us here is Scripture-memorization: feasting on the Word of God. We are clean though our adherence to God's Word (read John 15:3, 17:17, Eph. 5:26). Or see Philippians 4:8—"Finally, brethren, whatsoever things are pure...think on these things." Can there be anything purer than the Word of God? You are now fully equipped to combat the evil forces of the lustful mind. Upon entry of any such thoughts your refuge should be immediate reflection on verses of Scripture you have studied or memorized. "Think on these things!"

Psychologists, social anthropologists, and most experts in this capacity all agree and have proven that a man by nature is polygamous... that is, desirous of more than one woman. A man by his very nature at some time or another entertains the thought of an extra-marital affair. Whether or not it materializes beyond the state of curiosity or desire is relative to circumstances.

A very well-known evangelist, when confronted with the questions "What are the greatest temptations that face most evangelists?" replied, "Pride and women." Just imagine—to most Christians a calling that high would indicate a man being almost impregnable to the temptation of women. But, much to the contrary, we find that we (the heirs of salvation) will always have to contend with one of the faces of sin. Here I have to draw the line of distinction between understanding the subject and condoning it. My point in relation these facts to better understand (and not condone) some of the weaknesses found in man's network of desires, usually housed behind the subconscious doors of the "id," as will be discussed in the coming chapters.

Paul speaks of evil being ever-present with him (Rom. 7:18). This is to include evil thoughts, among other things. To do good is just not in him, to think good is just not part of the program of his fleshly nature. Yet he goes on to express in I Cor. 9:27 his firm stand in bringing his fleshly desires to a point of yielding to the will of God residing in the "inner man." That is to say, with all the sinful lusts that surround us and at times seem to almost drown us, we have at the same time an equal amount of power available to us to combat them. In Paul's concluding statement of his plight in Chapter 7 of Romans, he opens with, "Oh, wretched man that I am. Who shall deliver me from the body of this death?"—that is, the lust and corruption in his body. He concludes, "I thank God through Jesus Christ...." Victory comes through the person of Jesus Christ just by simply handing over the weaknesses of your nature to him and allowing him to be himself in you.

Yielding to sin after praying about deliverance from it is usually a psychological reaction as a result of the pressures of anticipated satisfaction-fulfillment. In other words, now that you have prayed about the grace to sustain you from any sinful act, the feeling for it can leave you. However, the spiritually-unoccupied mind begins to crave for it—so much so that you find yourself indulging.

Dedicated to the thousands of Christian singles
I was able to help and encourage.

(1980-2004)
Bro. Wes

Chapter I
The Threshold
Part I

"For which of you intending to build a tower, sitteth not down first, and counteth the cost...?"

Luke 14:28

Don't make the mistake of thinking God is just going to up and drop her right into your lap. If this does happen it is a very, very rare occasion. What worked for Adam was not programmed to work for you. With the law of averages working for him, Adam couldn't miss. Just think—when Eve was created there was only one man available for the preoccupation! God designed Eve for Adam, not as a specific individual, but as a woman. We sometimes like to feel that one man or one woman was specifically created for us, and I think it's wonderful when we can feel this way; but the idea is false. God designed or programmed one man for one woman on a subjective basis and not a personal one.

Proverbs 3:13 depicts the man's role as the initiator of a courtship. The question that now faces us is whether or not one should marry or stay single. "But and if thou marry, thou hast not sinned; and if a virgin marry, she hath not sinned. Nevertheless, such shall have trouble in the flesh: but I spare you." (I Cor. 7:28.) Throughout this entire chapter, Paul states two alternatives. The preferred one is to abstain from marriage. But look out—he warns in the latter part of verse 28—if you do marry, prepare to assume the trouble, cares, frustrations, etc.,

That go with marriage. You are now obligated to cope with these. Verses 33 and 34 become absolutely essential to your relationship. You must go to no end to satisfy your partner; this obligation comes at any cost. No price is too great. You weren't able to bear the status of remaining single (as Jesus said in Matt. 19:11), so the obligation of pleasing each other is paramount.

> X = < Y

Legend:

> - greater X- pleasing

< - lesser Y- trouble

This formula in reverse also works quite well:

< X = > Y

Except it be by specific directions from God, the option of marriage vs. celibacy is clearly contingent on one's ability at self-control and one's desire. As Paul so novelly puts it, to remain in a single state is preferred.

I Cor. 11:9—"Neither was the man created for the woman, but the woman for the man."

The motive for marriage becomes a cycle. The biological or sexual drives that will be discussed in the coming chapters motivate the male towards marriage. This is what Jesus talks about in Matt. 19:11—"… all men cannot receive this saying." Not all men—in fact, very few—are able to bear this type of physical restraint. And because of this, every man is exhorted to seek a wife rather than lust after a woman and/or burn in his desire for sexual satisfaction.

We read in Matt. 5:28 that a man who even looks at a woman and entertains the thought of sexual intercourse with her has sinned against God and his own body. Because of God's wonderful provisions in His creation-program, there is no need of falling into this sin. He created the woman for the man so that this need, among many other significant ones, could be satisfied, and so that in obtaining this satisfaction there would be a mutual love-cycle established between man and woman.

He has promised in His Word to keep our minds clean from sinful thoughts. Ps. 199:11—"Thy word have I hidden in my heart that I might not sin against thee." John 17:17—"Sanctify through thy truth, thy word is truth;" also John 15:3—"And his holy spirit to preserve us from straying into sinful activity."

The thought may seem a bit vulgar, but it is still a fact to contend with –that is, one of the major things that prompts a man towards marriage even beyond the point of companionship is sex. This is prefaced by man's biological drives (discussed in Chapter 4—"Personality Conflicts"). To prove this, examine the following statement. You cannot have love without sexual drive—impossible. Sex then becomes a part of the fulfillment of love. It is the epitome (highest height) of commitment. Love is the zenith of devotion.

As Christ loved the church and devoted his life to it, he receives as a result a total commitment (of the individual life) from the constituents that comprise the church. We can draw an analogy with husband and wife. As the husband imparts his love/devotion, he receives this total commitment (Sex) within the bonds of marriage. They both end up enjoying both elements of the formula (love and sex).

It is often said that a woman requires more love than sex, and that a man requires the opposite—more sex than love. The percentage for both fluctuates according to certain variables that pertain to both individuals. Both man and woman require love and sex in the cycle.

Bernard Talmey (M.D.) in his book on love expresses his views as follows: "Eros and libido are the two components of unusual love... libido represents the material pleasure enjoyed by the contact; eros represents the spiritual enjoyment experienced by the knowledge of loving and being loved. Libido is of a physical nature. Eros is a psychic phenomenon.... Libido is more a masculine sex trait, eros more feminine. For the ordinary man the libidinous part of love is the primary importance; when this emotion has been destroyed by some accident, he considers himself emasculated. He will never reveal the loss of his testicles, while a woman will openly and freely talk of an ovariotomy performed on her, although the loss of ovaries generally reduce the importance of experiencing orgasm, as the loss of the testicles does in men. She seems not to mind this loss, provided always that her eros has remained intact.... This woman rules over the man so long as he is in love. That is henpecked who came under his wife's authority from the beginning, by reason of his excessive sexual needs, and is continually kept under her rule by the same sensual needs. A man's dependence upon his wife can only be explained upon sensual basis. This is the reason why the woman is continually bent upon keeping the man's libido alive. Her constant desire is to influence him by her charms.

... Eros consists of two desires, to love and to be loved. The man is more anxious to love, the woman to be loved. She desires to feel that she is admired or, rather, coveted by men. Even a woman who, for moral or morbid reasons, renounces the libido will still have the desire to be admired and loved. This is all part of her feminine vanity."

It is not my intention to make this sound as if a woman's sole purpose is a sex outlet. On the contrary, both Greek and Hebrew words for "wife" in the Old and New Testaments strongly reflect the picture of a helpmate in every aspect.

Her job is so important and equally demanded that the Bible places high value on the woman who reflects all the virtuous qualities. "Her price is far above rubies."

As a result of the marital need that is created, the subsequent seek-and-find is given birth. This is sometimes done subconsciously. The desire for companionship and all of its components actively stimulates you. in Samson's case, he was of age to recognize his need of woman—after which he went to his parents, which was the custom of his day, to secure her (Judges 14:1, 2). In your case you begin taking care of this day by seeking and courting and marrying.

The basic prerequisite that the Bible requires is that the one to whom you wish to become joined be "in the Lord." This is the only essential spiritual must. Qualities of virtue are not mandatory. After all, you have to live with her. The only *physical* requisite (which is not essential must) is the aspect of compatibility. Two people should be of compatible mind if any degree of marriage success is to be expected. Amos 3:3—"Can two walk together, expect they be agreed?" A perfect example of such compatibility and singlemindedness is found in Act 5:4-10. Ananias and Sapphira were of the same mind, but *not in* the Lord.

Webster's definition of the word "compatibility" states that compatibility is the capability of coexisting in harmony. Note that. Not necessarily existing in harmony, but the capability of existing in harmony. So then compatibility doesn't necessarily have to be evidenced by functioning similarly in *everything*. But as long as the pattern of thinking is similar, the potential lends itself to the happiness of the marriage.

The Word of God records the experience of King Solomon having 700 wives and 300 legal girlfriends. The Bible goes further on to explain that God had made him the wisest man in Creation. If we examined Solomon's harem, we find it was comprised almost exclusively of foreign (pagan) women. The Bible further states that these women turned his heart from God: "Yet among many nations was there no king like him, who was beloved of his God, and God made him king over all Israel; *nevertheless, even him did foreign woman cause to sin.*" (Neh 13.26)

Can you imagine a man endowed with the greatest gift of wisdom from God's very own hand? And because of his affiliation with these pagan women, this wisdom was brought to nothing. "Be ye not unequally yoked together with unbelievers; for what fellowship hath righteousness with unrighteousness? And what communion hath light with darkness?" (2 Cor. 6:14)

None of us will ever be as wise as Solomon was. God had allowed these things to happen for a purpose, one of them being that we would learn and be inspired to follow His word of instruction into all truth. (Rom. 15:4).

This subsequently presents the entire spectrum of companionship, of which sex is a major component. Sex should be a "minor" ambition as well as by-product of a marriage, and not the goal. Too often one goes into this with such a high degree of sexual expectation that he or she can literally have a one-track mind. Marriage is not just for procreation or the usual sexual involvement that goes with it. It represents a type of relationship between Christ and the Church: the warmth of daily communion and fellowship—physical and spiritual—with each other, as a testimony to fellow-believers, the world, and loved ones.

God would have us further promote His plan of salvation through the communion, love and fellowship one should see in a Christian marriage.

Sex is very short-lived enjoyment. After those few moments of physical involvement and pleasure, the anxiety of pleasure, being fulfilled, dies. Multiply this times the number of involvements and you get a routine so blasé that you relate it to having breakfast, lunch or dinner. In the absence of mental, social or spiritual compatibility, there is no recourse to a common ground. You would have nothing else in common save the sexual pursuit and temporary satisfaction involved. This inevitably would be disastrous.

It's all too swift; it's over all too soon—
The quickened pace, the gasps, the final swoon,
The sudden dying down of flame and fire
The loosened limbs, the loss of all desire.
Let us control it; love is far more than
The itching heat of stray dog—or man.
—Petronius

What I'm emphatically suggesting here is that two newly-associated people place "major" spiritual emphasis on finding each other's areas of compatibility in such things as the patterns of thinking; behavior; art and music appreciation; spiritual appreciations, etc. Developing this kind of communication during the pre-marital stages is a very important part of preparation for all after-marriage activities. Take time to sit down with each other to discuss all topics of interest. Make it a point of searching out each other's reasonings behind expressed wishes; ambitions; interests; views; opinions; Scripture interpretations; etc. as a result of this, you will be able to come to a conclusion of compatibility versus incompatibility between you.

Part II

"Beloved, if our heart condemn us not, then have we confidence toward God."
1 John 3:21

There are many common questions faced· in the dating spectrum. One of the most complete and common questions is, "How far can I go?" Sex has confronted the young adult today as a major issue.

Research has reflected basic differences between males and females and their attitudes toward sex. A study of the motives of college students who had premarital intercourse showed that the fellows' number-one reason for going all the way was to gain physical pleasure. Curiosity was second. Only 5% gave "love" as their motive. On the other hand, girls overwhelmingly went "all the way" because they thought they loved their fellows. Another interesting reaction comes from fellows and girls who believe it is okay to go all the way on a date. What are their reasons? For the girl it was "I love him." But the big reason for the fellows was

"I like it." Other motives behind sexual involvement to the young male adult would be proving masculinity to himself, the girl, and other fellows within his social crowd. On the other hand, the young female adult feels loved and needed-a comforting feeling that is often short-lived.

A very interesting observation here is that many young people get involved, not for lust's sake, but because of the genuine growth of love. This is when we allow our physical reactions to compete with our emotions and feelings for that one.

Paul speaks of a deeper love that goes beyond feelings and emotions, one that maintains loyalty at any cost-a love that cannot rest on foundation of sensations, emotions, or feelings, because these all change. In summary, it is a love that rests on purpose and resolve, reflecting a total commitment to seek only the best for the one loved; not our feelings, but our intentions to do what is best for the other.

Are you uncertain as to what is best in your relationship before God? You have been given a spiritual conscience, fed by the knowledge of the Word of God. It is our duty to choose conscience over impulse. The Christian is exhorted to live by faith. Anything that is void of faith is sin. Therefore, if there are any doubts about what you're doing, you have no business doing it. "And he who doubts is condemned" (Rom. 14:23) because he has not fulfilled his action through faith. Faith doesn't doubt. In context of this chapter, which refers to partaking, for our purposes we'll substitute the thought-involvement (instead of partaking). Involvement without faith (unassurance, wavering) is sin. " ... to him that knoweth to do good and doeth it not, to him, it is sin" Games 4:17). "That which is without faith is sin." (Rom. 14:23).

Too often emphasis has been placed on physical attraction. Male sees female-nice face, attractive physique, hence nice personality. Or she sees a handsome fellow, perhaps nice height or build and (usually because of the shortage of men) nice fellow. From here the physical attraction leads to physical involvement; first, holding hands; then kissing; necking, petting; and subsequently as far as sexual intercourse. The above emphasis was placed on satisfying the physical requests of the first nature. I like to refer to the motivations of this fleshly nature as "the call of the wild." "Who shall deliver me from this body, I thank God through Jesus Christ." Paul acknowledges his weakness :111d goes on triumphantly to joyously recognize victory in Jesus. We have the same access.

If emphasis is overwhelmingly placed on these "minors," and little if any placed on the "majors," a relationship will result as a one-sided objective involvement.

Because of the communication poverty that arises with the pursuit of the minors, one will detect a widening communication gap after the early stages of marriage. Major in the "majors" and you cannot go wrong. If you come through with a good average on your compatibility quota, the "minors" will automatically fall in line. After the first encounter that physically attracted you to each other, relate predominantly to the "majors" and the "minors" will inevitably (at the right time) follow—because it takes no effort; it's natural. Develop the spiritual, intellectual, and social aspects of compatibility. The physical should be left as the topping on the cake, obtainable only after marriage.

Chapter I
Part II: The Threshold
[ADDENDUM]

Fast forward 10 years later, I was now blessed with graduate degrees. One in clinical Psy (SUNY/Grow Institute) and one from New York Theological Seminary. In 1980 I founded Christian Dating Service International. The concept was to build Christian families worldwide by introducing Christian singles of the same and similar faith to each other (1980-2004). I was astonished at how fast this took off within a year we were reaching major radio and T.V. markets with our commercials these numbers were bolstered 4 years later in 1985 when Pat Robinson of the 700 club sent a film crew up to our mansion headquarters to do our story. I was told this added 96 million viewers to our existing traffic. I recall a time when a burgeoning ESPN and the weather channel came to us for advertising support and I wrote a special contract to encourage and facilitate their early efforts. This activity and success was all pre-internet. 15 years later the internet represented a second explosion of success. What you see today as "Christian Mingle" and "e-Harmony" is an extension of what I pioneered (1980-2004). In spite of the success this phenomena was then met with some pushback from a few pastors who felt that relationships should just happen natural. So there was somewhat of a stigma attached to the concept. Would you be desperate enough to seek a dating service?? Of course today in 2020 internet dating is a norm. In the dialogue I had with pastors along the way particularly with mailings I would as ask the question, "What is the most important decision any person could make in this life??" And follow up with "Inviting Jesus Christ into a personal relationship," At which point most would agree. Then I would ask, "What is the second most important decision of a person's life?" And say, "Would you agree that deciding the person that you would want to spend your life with??" The justification for having a dating service for Christians now made sense. The response from Pastor's was almost unanimous. This resulted in hundreds of pastors endorsing the concept, resulting in the success of CDS.

Through God's guidance I was able to facilitate tens of thousands of Christian singles over that quarter century (1980-2004) into relationships and many hundreds of marriages to the Glory of God. It would take a book to express the hundreds of adventures and miracles that came out of CDS; which even brought me to the White House (see short bio). What I didn't expect was the influx of an older generation. Those who were widows, widowers or divorced over the age of 50 (50-85). Guidance here was both different and challenging. For this older generation the world had changed so much. I became very sympathetic a "DEAR ABBEY," to the concerns and issues of thousands of older Christian singles who wanted Godly guidance. This was now a fulltime commitment I deeply enjoyed.

THE KEY

For both young and older Christian singles the key to relationship success was communication. I left off in chapter I part II the last paragraph "communication poverty." Here we can address that with empirical observation from CDS. Our modus operandi of covering the United States was to section off the country and tri-state areas. 70 percent of the matching took place outside of the NY-NJ tri-state area. Clients would have the option of requesting even further distances for referrals. What I found interesting was the thousands of testimonials we received discussing how rich relationships matured through **letter writing**. This lead to substantive phone calls and deeper insights when writing. I will go as far as saying most of those relationships and marriages were outside of their respective states. The months of writing developed a communication pattern that left no stone unturned as to who this perspective mate was. In my general counsel to the membership I stressed this mode of communication to those who lived in the same city. IT WORKED!!!

Establishing this kind of communication foundation prior to marriage would be ideal. However, for those already married, it's not too late to begin fostering a letter writing pattern. That along with dates set aside with each other is doable, even in old age. One can dream about what could be, and work to make it happen. Keep in mind love and forgiveness are the strongest pillars of our Faith. This works if you are a member of God's family a genuine born again believer, if you are not, or not sure, God offers you a free invitation to join His family. See appendix 1. *Jesus says I have come that they may have life, they may have life more abundantly* (John 10:10). This includes marriage relationships into old age.

Chapter II
Journeying

"Whoso findeth a wife findeth a good thing."
Proverbs 18:22

I think it is necessary here to restate the will of God in this matter of securing a wife or husband. God has laid down only one requirement for your choosing a partner, and that is that you be "in the Lord" (I Cor. 7:39). He has granted us the liberty to choose and refuse to our liking. Because we were not all created with the same personalities, it would be ludicrous to assume that any two, even Christian, people could get along living together. This is why seeking personality-compatibility is so important. *This is "God's will" for your life*, marrying "in the Lord."

Now, if you are not sure of whom, and you want explicit direction concerning this matter, then you should commit this to unceasing prayer. We can rest in the assurance that He who made us knows our every need; and in honestly confiding in His direction and strength, we cannot help but secure His will for our lives.

Let us at this point examine God's will. I believe there are two aspects of God's will we have to contend with. There is God's "directive will" and His "permissive will" that is, to be more explicit, what He wants· and that which He allows. Let's consider for discussion an example of the following prayers·:

Example #1: "Lord, I love ___ Make it possible (endorse) him/her: to be 'my; life partner." This is usually prayed after you've made up "your will" for what should be.

Example #2: "Lord, I find myself of age and am desirous of a life partner. If this is in line with your will for my life, direct my heart towards that one which would complete your design and will for my life." If you really desire God's direction towards "that one," you must be equally willing to wait for His time to reveal "that one," you must be equally willing to wait for His time to reveal "that one."

One difference in this second prayer is that you haven't preconceived a partner, but rely expectantly on God's direction. I firmly believe that in seeking the Kingdom of God and His righteousness first even these needs will be taken care of in the right way in His time. Isaac was in the field at eventide taking care of God's business in providing a wife (she was on the way—read Gen. 24:63). This is how God works, "Seek ye first the kingdom of God, and all these things shall be added unto you" (Luke 12:31).

The first prayer suggests one having sought his or her own will first, then asking God to put His approval on it. The second prater is seeking God's will first and waiting for results. One very important point to realize is that, if we're persistent enough, God will grant us "our will" even though it may conflict with what He wants for us. But we will always end up paying for it. An example of this can be found in Psalms 106:15—"...and he gave them their requests but sent leanness to their soul." We will pay for it in the long run. With this survey of thoughts, I think our basis for the understanding of "wills" is clear.

Let's take another look at Proverbs 18:22. "Whoso of the Lord." This verse is very often misunderstood. The proper reading of this text as found in the amplified Old Testament is, "He who finds a *true* wife finds a good thing and obtains the favor of the Lord." Proverbs 19:14 further confirms this. "Houses and riches are the inheritance from fathers, but a wise understanding and prudent wife is from the Lord." (Both taken from the amplified translation.) Do you see the difference? Not just having any wife is the same as obtaining favor from the Lord. Yours is the responsibility, among other things, to look into these qualities. The Bible puts women into two categories: Virtuous and on-virtuous. A book could be written to further expound on these qualities, found in Proverbs 31:10. This is not to say that a woman of lesser virtue would be incompatible to live with. But it would be extremely helpful in looking for these qualities, found in Proverbs 31:10. This is not to say that a woman of lesser virtue would be incompatible to live with. But it would be extremely helpful in looking for these qualities and obtaining them.

I think it would be fairly easy to detect this pattern of behavior for the qualities of both virtuous and non-virtuous women during the months of courtship. Love can easily hide any shortcoming, if you so desire it. Otherwise, if you lift your eyelids for a few moments, perhaps you may get a better assessment of this new dimension found in the character-pattern of your intended. In the final analysis the choice (of each other) is yours.

Many times we can grow impatient thinking that God is never

going to come through. If you were to consider the average length of time a man and wife live together (approximately 30 years), I would say the wait would be well worth it. Can you imagine spending 30 years in misery just because you couldn't wait a few years? It is far, far better to "miss" (the opportunity of marrying by a hasty decision) than to make a "mistake" (which would cost you something for the rest of your life). Too often, though believers have pursued a social involvement with too serious an objective contemplated. During a courtship, taking all things into consideration, this should be done in such a natural tone so as not to force the issue. We should look forward to dating as a casual thing, not always seeking to foster an eternal relationship. A relationship should develop naturally. Anything other than that could cause unnatural balance in the stages of life after marriage.

God designed sex as part of the human structure. It is something to be admired and loved as much as any other physiological function of our humanity. Sex was designed as a gift-package to be presented to a couple holy matrimony, to be exercised exclusively in the realm of married life. The trouble comes when we violate God's design and purpose. We expose ourselves to the act of intercourse prior to marriage and wonder why our minds wander and lust after the thought of someone else, even after many years of marriage.

When we become deeply affectionate to that one prior to marriage and continue it to the point of getting sexually involved—Boom! Pow! Bang! Something happens, and that one never "makes the scene" all the way (marriage). But, perhaps, also gone with that one are the gratifying sexual experiences you may never consistently enjoy again—not to become the unhappy recipient of your own disobedience. Now, when your potential husband comes along, you shudder (this goes for you too, fellow!). the guilt-complex sets in and maybe you're sorry. In the event that you marry, you may find that this experience isn't as enjoyable as the ones in "sin camp" experienced with your departed(s)!

Of course, at this point one must realize that there are many variables that can make these statements a little truer or give them less validity. If this is true, a greater amount of effort will be necessary in the sexual habits and adjustments of the new couple.

Even if we shy away from the standards of Scripture regarding pre-marital sex, logic alone should reveal the tragedy of this vice. If as a woman you become sexually involved outside of marriage, the chances are that 3 out of 5 times you will become sexually attached to one of your first three suitors.* perchance something happens and you don't marry him; let's just suppose he walks out on you. after all, he's been getting what he wanted and now someone comes along that looks a little better. You have no legitimate ties to him, so you lose without being able to fabricate any legal defenses. The man you are going to marry comes along. You may or may not continue your sexual ventures with him. In most cases he's looking for the virtues of virginity as priority-item number one. You may be able to assert the usual, "I made a mistake"; or, "I was young and easily misled." But—the big "but"—you have been exposed to sex and you have enjoyed the results of it.

In most cases you have gotten used to the bodily communion of "that one." Do you think for one minute it will be easy to adjust to another human being, considering his difference in sexual exposure; sexual appetite; genital structure; sexual experience (if any); overall attitudes; and temperament, as opposed to your background of experiences? You may find falling short of all of these satisfactions you experienced with your previous experiences remains a constant threat to your "memory" facilities. This especially true in the face of discontent and depression.

Wouldn't it all have been better if you hadn't gotten involved in the first place? You became adjusted to one man. In the event of short-lived sexual frustrations, you both worked towards dual satisfaction. Here there is no sentimental desire for someone who might be consistently better. I'm sure we can all appreciate this vast difference.

There should be full and open confession before each other of these things prior to marriage. It may be painful to admit, but it will save suspicion, mistrust, etc. in the years to follow when these things are found out.

All is not lost! In spite of your failing into sin prior to marriage, upon acknowledging your sin and being genuinely penitent before God, your heavenly Father is faithful and just to forgive you of all prior acts.

We must realize that the first unit of fellowship was not the church or school, but the family. God wants our family life to be a success. The very fact that a husband-and-wife relationship is a type of Christ and the Church further evidences the serious nature of coveting a successful and happy marriage. This is a testimony to be maintained before the children, fellow believers, and the world. In spite of your shortcomings, He wants your marriage relationship to glorify and exemplify Him. To do this effectively, He must become the foundation of your marriage. "Except the Lord build the house, they labor in vain that build it" (Psalms 127:1). It is the man's rightful place to commit the marriage and establishment of the home into God's hands. As the head of the house, he should be the guardian of this responsibility, daily asking for the wisdom and guidance to build on the foundation of God's will. Though the years may roll by, don't ever get to the point of thinking that you have reached the pinnacle of success and thereby declare independence by deviating from this responsibility.

Chapter II
Journeying
[ADDENDUM]

In this addendum I think it's appropriate in this courtship/dating chapter to take a moment to step back and examine who we are as individuals. God created us as a tri-part entity (1 Thessalonians 5:23): "...And I pray God your whole spirit and soul and body be preserved blameless unto the coming of the Lord Jesus Christ."

Spirit (Godconciousness); Soul/Mind (Thoughts, Emotions, Will) and body (the 5 senses), according to Romans 7:15-25 and 8:13 the Spirit is at war with our flesh. There is no war between the Spirit and flesh to non-Christians. The Soul is also at war with our Flesh. This is a daily and sometimes hourly battle.

Our Spirit domain is the most important of these three entities. This is our Godconciousness, created in all human beings. It was designed to accommodate God's Holy Spirit upon request—personal. This is not automatic. Romans 8:9: "...If any man hath not the spirit of Christ, he is none of his." You must request membership to enter God's family to experience this honor. See Appendix 1. Jesus proclaims in John 4:24: "God is a Spirit and they that worship him, must worship Him in the Spirit and truth." When God created us in His image, this Spirit domain is that image. God has given us a will, the opportunity to choose our way or His ways—CHOICE!! He did not want robots. And He will not violate this principle of CHOICE. If we choose God, then He comes into this Spirit domain within us with His Holy Spirit and resides there (the new birth). Each part of the tri-part entity that we are has an appetite a compulsion to be filled or satisfied. Now in the Spirit entity this appetite yearns to be fed and nurtured. The only menu is the Word of God and prayer. The Word of God feeds our inner spirit. Prayer nurtures it. As Christians we face three mortal enemies daily: the World, the Flesh, and the Devil (see Appendix 3). Bolstering our inner man/Spirit with the Word and prayer is the only way to defeat these enemies.

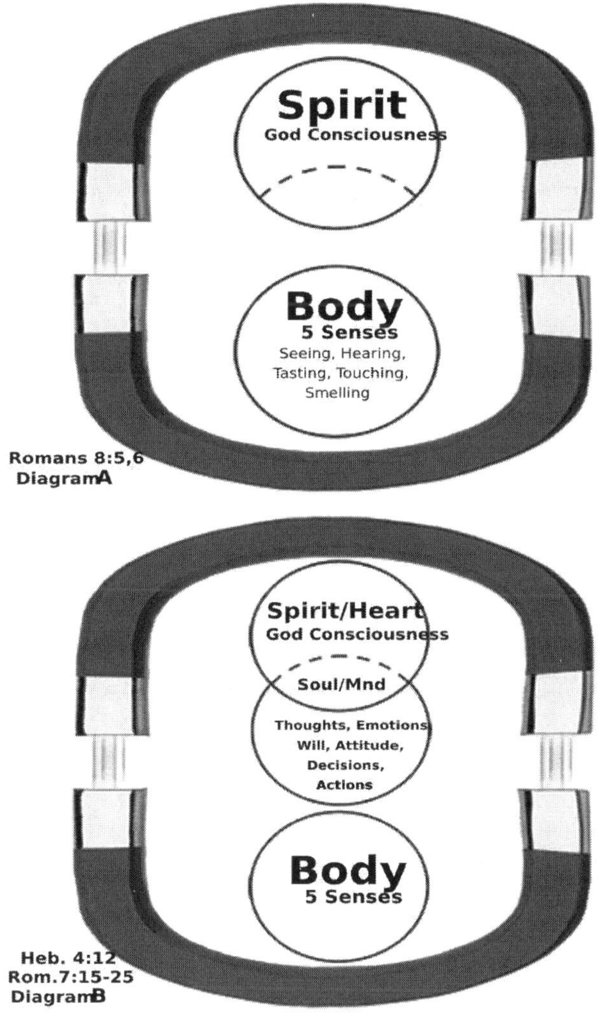

Would you consider making it a practice of eating just once a week? And yet some Christians are guilty of doing that Spiritually. Having one spiritual meal a week on Sunday morning. Usually skipping prayer and Bible study during the week is a norm for most Christians. This is the reason for the powerless church we have today compared to the early church.

There are 1,440 minutes in our daily cycle. Would it be too much to set aside 15 of those 1,440 minutes for fellowship with our Heavenly Father? Giving thanks for our life, health, strength and healing and the opportunity to present our request; and just 10 minutes to let him speak to you through His Word??? Church prayer meetings and Bible studies would be enhanced if you did your part. The non-Christian is also endowed with this inner Spirit domain that desires to be fed. Their resources are: self, a person, money, fame, alcohol, drugs, et cetera, et cetera, et cetera—all which lasts only temporarily. All short lived. Non-Christians are sitting ducks for Satan. They have no defense against Satan, the Devil. This is evidence by a growing prison system, overwhelmed psychologist and psychiatrists offices, and thousands of research findings, "I heard voices..." 2 Timothy 2:26: "And that they may recover themselves out of the snare of the Devil, who are taken captive by him at his will."

Have you ever found yourself asking the question "Did that thought come from me or was that God speaking to me??" The reason for this is found in Hebrews 4:12: "For the Word of God is piercing and powerful and sharper than even a two-edge sword piercing to the dividing asunder the Soul and Spirit...." There is overlap between the Spirit and the Soul. They are so uniquely intertwined that it takes the Word of God: time and prayer to answer that question. God wants us to know there is a clear distinction between the Soul Mind and Spirit/Heart. It is confirmed on two occasions that there would be no man before or after Solomon endowed with his wisdom given by God. Listen to the public blessing and admonition his father David gives him before conveying his throne to him. 1 Chronicles 28:9: "And thou

Solomon my son, know thou the God of thy father, and serve Him with a perfect heart and with a willing mind; for the Lord searcheth all hearts, and understandeth all the imaginations of the thoughts...." While he remained obedient, he became the wealthiest of all beings, when he disobeyed, his fall was more profound than his rise. And Revelation 2:23: "...I am he who searches the mind (The New Scofield Study Bible and ESV) and heart; and I will give to each of you according to your works," everything that's not of God. This is immediately engaged by the mind/soul. When filtered here, there are three choices, one Godly response of the Spirit/God consciousness. Two, humanistic response, just do the right thing/society norms. Three, body's natural response, yield to the stimuli. If the Spirit is not well fed with Godly input, then you end up with number 3.

The story is told of an American Indian explaining good vs. bad to his grandson. He explains we all have a good and bad wolf that is part of us. And further that they always fight. The young lad asked, "Who wins the fight?" The grandfather replied, "The wolf we feed."

Mind over Matter

All of us have heard stories of impossible feats being done that defy explanation and logic. The example of the mother who conjures up abnormal strength to lift a 4,000-pound vehicle off of her child—mind over matter. Hundreds of such stories unfold year after year. I was amazed to recently Google the subject matter and discover that science, Para science and medicine caught up with this phenomena. This ranges from Psychokinesis (the mind's ability to move objects), to actual miracles bringing along a host of scientific platforms. A consensus among scientists is that we use less than 12 percent of our brain. So, even science admits to the power within the mind, our souls.

Conclusion

The world can rally around mind over matter. As Christians we have the edge. We have Spirit over Mind over Matter: "Greater is He that is in you, than he that is in the world" (1 John 4:4). Praise God. Now equipped with this information there is no excuse to not have a successful marriage if you follow God's rules. With this understanding of you let us proceed. Let's pick up from Proverbs 18:22: "Whoso findeth a wife findeth a good thing, and obtaineth favor of the Lord." This verse is very often misunderstood. The proper reading of this text is found in the Amplified Old Testament: "He who finds a true wife finds a good thing and obtains favor of the Lord" and also Proverbs 19:14: "...A prudent wife is from the Lord." The Bible puts women in two categories, virtuous and non-virtuous. Both can and will marry. However, under the Christian umbrella the virtuous women will fare better she will want to do and live God's Word, guaranteeing a successful marriage, barring any unforeseen flukes. Marriage is not a 50/50 proposition which is the world's position vis-à-vis the Christians. Ironically, the wife will receive 100 percent of the benefits by simply adhering to God's direction through His Word. In this chapter we're dealing with the premarital stage where you have the opportunity to be prayerful, pensive, and objectively observant.

To the female prospect I say read Chapter 3 and especially Chapter 4 and examine the feminist theology position and ask yourself, "Can I commit to what God is expecting of me and serving my husband? Or has societal conditioning relegated me to its 50/50 position??" Remember, you will have God's help here if you wish to continue this relationship His way. Be honest with yourself. Don't even think to yourself, "I'll work it out in marriage." You will not change him!!! This is your opportunity in this dress rehearsal stage of careful decision making. To the male prospect I suggest you read Chapter 3, "Love," and Chapter 4, "Marriage." Can you commit to being consistent in staying in the Word of God to better understand and learn Godly character and this woman He may be giving you? It is obviously important to get a commitment from her as to whether or not she will be a conformist.

Both of you should decide on a counselor or two in this important endeavor. The persons should be spiritually attuned to the Word of God. Degrees here mean little. Pastors and deacons and deaconesses are good prototypes but don't overlook the older sisters or mothers of the church. Titus 2:3-4: "... That the age women...teach the young women to be sober minded, to love their husbands...." IQ is not determined by education. I know of people who hadn't had the opportunity of obtaining a degree yet had an unquestionable high IQ, and comprehension level. Psychologists and Psychiatrists are okay; however, their contributions are usually of a secular order versus Godly counsel in most cases. If you can find a "Christian" Psychologist or Psychiatrist that's a win-win. Since the word "Christian" can carry a relative status quo don't be afraid to ask about their faith and how their faith influences their counsel. 1 John 4:1: "Beloved, believe not every Spirit, but test the Spirits whether they are from God; because many false prophets are gone out into the world." Counseling is a gift. The institution of counseling can also be learned. I give you the examples of Steve Harvey vs. Dr. Phil. With all of Dr. Phil's degrees there is no contest in his counseling abilities compared to the lesser educated (high school plus some college) Steve Harvey. No comparison. None. To see how God has changed this once talented but rowdy struggling and broke individual into the successful titan and example of God's grace he is today, is inspiring, I'm so proud of you, Steve.

Many years ago (1970), Dr. Jay Adams wrote the book *Competent to Counsel*, where he expounded on the concept of not necessarily needing degrees for effectiveness in counseling. Since then he's expanded his ministry worldwide to train missionaries and church leaders for effective counseling in the country of their ministry.

Chapter III
LOVE

"Many waters cannot quench love,
neither can the floods drown it."
(S. of S. 8:7)

One of the greatest mistakes projected by either partner going into a marriage contract is the fallacy of thinking one can alter the other's personality. Many couples accept the attitude of habits of their potential life-partners with the hidden preconceived notion of "I'll change that after we're married"—only to be confronted with much disappointment in the years to follow.

How many times can you remember hearing, "I married him/her because he/she said he/she loved me so much"? Yes, basically, someone is trying to get without the attitude of willingly giving (in spite of getting). I don't believe that all the books in the world could relate the specific problems and adjustments that can give rise to dissatisfaction between partners in marriage. Before diagnosing the variety of problems that exist, I think we should get a better idea of the part played by the cure—that is, love.

Every method, therapy and application discussed in this volume indubitably revolves around this four-letter word. Perhaps there have been more books, songs and philosophies written about this topic than any other.

The Greeks had three different words to express this. One of the highest emotions is expressed by the word *"agapai."* It is love the man feels for God, parents or country, founded upon worship, adoration and gratitude. *"Philei"* designates the love founded on sympathy and liking, such as the love of humanity, or hobby-interest. The last was expressed by the word *"eroi."* This is love based on sex-attraction.

The manifestations of attachment may have as its origin selfish interest. They may be given in exchange for the expectancy of favors to come. Fondness, liking and attachment even to the degree of committing suicide upon the loss of the person coveted, may not be true love. An example of this is the man who commits suicide after losing all of his wealth. Yet money is not loved for its own sake, but for the power it possess of procuring the means for enjoyment.

I don't suppose I will ever become an authority on the academic philosophies and theories engineered by the great minds that have expounded on this subject matter; taking into account the differences of opinion are evidenced in the respective reading-materials of these men. Therefore, my refuge for a sound and infallible definition of love will be taken from the Word of God. First Corinthians, 13th Chapter, expatiates the meaning of love superbly. In fact, it encompasses the Greek differentiations mentioned. For the sake of clarity, we will read verses 4-8 from the NASBNT translation:

"4. Love is patient, love is kind, and is not jealous; love does not brag and is not arrogant;
5. does not act unbecomingly; it does not seek its own, is not provoked, does not take into account a wrong suffered;
6. does not rejoice in unrighteousness, but rejoices with the truth;
7. bears all things, believes all things, hope all things, endures all things.
8. Love *never* fails...."

Love is all these things. It extends to the zenith of willingness to lay down one's life—"Greater love hath no man..." (John 15:13)—for his-her partner.

Think deeply on this! Is your feeling for you partner (or intended partner) characterized by these points? Take each definition individually and weigh it against any or all the experiences you have encountered with your spouse. *Example:* "Love is not easily provoked." How many times have you failed? "...believes all things." How many times have you expressed lack of confidence in him or him?

We were not made perfect; we all fail. And in recognizing our failures we should be more-prone towards asking for God's interventions into our shortcomings—to become our strength where we are weak. We should earnestly acknowledge our failures and ask God to be God in us through His son, thereby radiating all the qualities of love through us, and subsequently to our loved one.

Let's go a step further and envision the most provoking and contemptible act that is thought conceivable for our wife or husband to be involved with. Is it conceivable that in that state of failure your love transcends the fault to the point of forgiveness? Solomon said that love is as strong as the grave. God help us each one to covet the power that is available in love, and to manifest this openly to our respective partners. To love secretly is to destroy the confidence if your partner in you. One can only read your actions and behavior to evaluate your feelings towards them. If true feelings are hidden and not expressed in your behavior, and those feelings happen to be love, how can you expect one to know this? "Open rebuke is better than secret love" (Pr. 27:5).

I think we have glimpsed enough of a meaning in this chapter to transpose it into actual everyday practice.

Pre-Hang-Ups

"Take us the foxes, the little foxes, that spoil the vines; for our vines have tender grapes."

S. of S. 2:15

Once upon a time there was a certain man who planted a vineyard and grew the finest grapes. He kept the vineyard as a good keeper would, anticipating the abundance of these delicious grapes. By and by he found that, with all the attention he had given the fruit, its growth was being hindered and partially ravished. After several weeks of investigation he found that sly foxes were feeding on the tender branches, and he set forth to build a fence immediately. After a while he found his hindrance to still be quite evident. Upon further investigation he found that tiny foxes had found the small openings and were imitating their elders in feeding on these tender grapes.

Let's consider a marriage to be a vineyard. The husband and wife will be the vines. The factors that represent happiness will be the grapes (e.g. getting along together; feeling secure; sex satisfaction, etc.) The foxes, both large and small, will represent the destructive factors in your marriage. Remembering that the marriage represents the relationship between Christ and the Church, and that God would further relate His plan of salvation through the means of the family, we can then appreciate why Satan will inevitably seek to put these foxes into disastrous motion. Satan is the enemy of God and His people, and of all that represents God and his righteousness. It is his business to gain a foothold and possible victory in the lives of the Christian couple. But is also our responsibility to make Christ our defense in countering all of Satan's assaults with the determination of being victorious.

Any Christian husband or wife who pensively thinks on these things must come to the conclusion that wherever there are symptoms of a sickness, there must be causes for them. And if there is enough concern on your part, you will make inquiries into the difficulties and try to change them (for the better, of course).

I must once again apologize as we enter this chapter for the brevity of examples, as they can be innumerable in marriage situations. However, let's peek at a few!

"The Little Things"

One component of love is patience—more tolerance towards one's partner. This end-result should be a total display of all the other partner's shortcomings. Love is biased in this way. The target of one's love is treated specially.

The absence of these qualities can be evidence quite easily. The disdain and contentious attitude over your partner's mannerisms; the mistrust and lack of confidence towards one's mater—"I can't take it anymore; I'm ready to quit;" the constant feeling of neglect and being ignored. All these show a lack of love. The lovable woman needs never to be uncertain of who she is and her place I her husband's life. She knows what her values are and feels a high degree of self-acceptance. To this end, she is a very confident person. the faith or trust that one exercises towards a spouse can be likened to the faith (belief) or non-faith (unbelief), that a sinner exercises towards God. Without this faith there exists a death in fellowship and communion between God and man. Without faith in your partner, the marriage will die. Don't be fooled by thinking that all couples who are physically together are experiencing this warm and trusting relationship. Many of these marriages are only seemingly well-put-together bodies on the surface, but full of dead men's bones underneath. Faith and trust are major components of love, without which a marriage cannot long endure. Each partner plays a major role in working towards securing everything that will build faith and trust in each other. It's only natural that, as human beings, we have habits and certain mannerisms that become a part of us. After a while they even begin to characterize us. Many of them may even create feelings of scorn among observing parties. However, this should never characterize the feeling of the spouse. Love also hides multitude of these little faults. We don't become annoyed over these little things. Our love and allegiance to our respective mates transcends and supersedes them.

As Christians we can look into a deeper aspect of the role played by personality. The Bible plainly states that any man being in Christ is a new creature and that all (old) things are passed away. This means the whole former attitude, ways and personality should be deceased. And the residence of the Lord Jesus in the form of the Holy Spirit has now been made a part of this "new" individual. The object at this point is to yield ourselves to the leading of the holy spirit within us, that we may develop to be more and more like Jesus.

What was His personality? Yes, a picture of love, and all the virtues that go with it. As Paul puts it, "The life that I now live, it's not me, but Christ who is living in me." This is to say that nothing is seen of Paul as a person, but Christ so dominates his life that one looking on could only see Christ living, operating and functioning in this Apostle's life. "He that hath begun a good work in you is faithful and just to continue it till the day of Christ." From the time one's regeneration one can faithfully trust God to continue His work of saving us from SIN—SELF—and SATAN. We now have the privilege of handing over our rotten, imperfect personalities (on a daily basis) to Him and asking Him to live His holy person though us.

The saddest dilemma Christians can find themselves in is the failure to recognize their shortcomings and honestly present them to the Father. Isn't this a marvelous provision? One which stands in defiance of medical research, psychology and psychiatry, and all of man's wisdom?

We have got to be willing to acknowledge self—that is, our attitudes, personalities, etc.—and yieldingly give them into His care, that by His occupancy in our place, God will be glorified by others seeing this spirit of Christ in us.

Chapter III
Love
[ADDENDUM]

Eros love: ancient Greeks define this as feelings of erotic desire, pointing to sexual passion; brought on by an initial and soulful appreciation, not necessarily a "physical" attraction to that other. It could be an attraction of the soul (Proverbs 27:19). We can safely call that chemistry if it is mutual. One of the saddest things in the human experience is rejection; when those initial feelings of Eros love are not returned. Everyone has experienced this. I recall an episode years ago on the *Arsenio Hall Show* where he was interviewing Eddie Murphy, who was at the height of his fame. The subject of love came up and he openly admitted several rejections he had experienced in his dating life. Even among movie stars the wealthy and the famous, this phenomena is common. If you are in a pre-marriage stage and there's not even a hint of interest from the person you've fallen in love with, you are not alone. Millions have been there, past, present, and there will be future. This is more common than you think. I'll borrow one of my mother's favorite sayings, "Good go, better come." Rejection is part of life. Our comforter, the Holy Spirit, is here to help. You would be amazed to discover how ambidextrous He is. There is no pain like love pain. Or hurt, like love hurt. There were two respective occasions in my life where I had to call on the Holy Spirit to take away the love I had for two individuals who did not want to follow the road I was on. I used to think the concept "die of a broken heart" was an old wives' fable. Life experience has made me a believer. Thank God for his Holy Spirit.

My favorite illustration of "love" comes from the Bible scholar Kenneth S. West. The setting is John Chapter 21. Jesus had been crucified and risen. The disciples were having a pity party. Their leader was gone; Verse 3, "I go fishing." What Peter was saying is I'm going back to my trade, my vocation, what I loved. The disciples chime in: "We're going with you.," The destiny of mankind was at stake here. The 3 years Jesus had spent in discipling and training would have been lost. Had there been no divine intervention there would be no church, no fellowship of God's people, no witnesses to carry on God's mission. Jesus sees this from heaven, races down through eternity into time to salvage the mission. They had fished all night and caught nothing. Meanwhile, Jesus is preparing breakfast on the shore and calls out, "Have you caught any fish (already knowing the answer)?" After breakfast Jesus confronts Peter in the presence of the disciples and asks, "Do you love me more than these? Do you love me more than these disciples? Do you love me more than these disciples love me? Do you love me more than these fish?" Examining the context closely, the bottom line is, "Do you love me more than the fish?" Your work, your vocation, your love. The Lord uses the word Agapeo the first two times he questions Peter, and Phileo the last time he asked Peter whether he loves him. Agapeo is used in various forms in the New Testament about 320 times. It is a love called out of a person's heart...a love of preciousness...a love of prizing...a love of "devotion" verses "emotion" that comes from the heart. Agape love is the ultimate love, a love that goes beyond the call of duty, the love of devotion verses emotion.

Sister, if you are in pre-marriage status, I strongly recommend you look at the Agape model and ask yourself, "Can I see myself potentially making that kind of total commitment to my intended???" And if not, run!!!

If already in a marriage relationship and you are a born-again Christian, you can ask your heavenly father for this love and he will gladly impart this to you as you obey Him in all elements in fellowship with Him. If you are not a born-again believer or are not sure, we invite you to become a part of God's family; go to Appendix 1. Here, by your sincere commitment to God you can join His family by faith. Over one thousand promises and benefits await you on your commitment. And the tools and knowhow to kindle this kind of love will be a fun project from both the Word of God, your newfound creativity and thousands of counselors and pastors waiting to help.

Chapter IV
MARRIAGE

"Two are better than one because they have a good reward for their labor; for if they fall, the one will lift up his fellow. But woe to him that is alone when he falleth; for he hath not another to help him up."

Ecc. 4:9, 10

If one were to take a mental note of all the scriptural as well as other guidelines available to Christians, dealing with the design of a successful marriage, such a one would be totally discourage when confronted with the countless number of failures seen. How can this be with such a wealth or resource? Perhaps this question can be answered in many ways. To do this effectively, we would have to examine some of the underlying causes.

Selfish Motives for Marriage

These can range from a mutual business proposition to the glorified hope of the material benefit to be gained in the marriage. Whether it be status; money; escape from lifetime loneliness; or otherwise, the chief attitude is "What's in it for me? How much can I get out of it?"

Here once again is the seeking to get—parasitical disposition of feeding on the promises of the partner without the intent of imparting one's entire self, void of any selfish reciprocations. To the woman it could be status; the difference between being an old maid or wife; security; a compensating factor (that is, "I couldn't get '*X*' so '*Y*' is the next best thing");or perhaps yielding to the current of the social fad—everyone is getting married, so why not? To the man it could be merely sexual gratification based on the attractive physical features alone of his intended partner; an escape from loneliness; money' or the satisfaction of topping the competition. Of course, for both sexes there can be many other reasons. Any two people who are contemplating marriage should carefully evaluate their motives before final commitment.

Personality Conflicts

As human beings, part of our physiological makeup is our "self," and our personality is a component of this. Our personality is an outward expression of our inner motivations. The Bible tells us "...as he (a man) thinketh in his heart, so is he." (Pr. 23:7) In the eyes of the psychologist the everyday man *cannot* change his personality; neither can psychotherapy. The purpose of psychotherapy is to enable one to resolve conflicts and cope with personality traits that are reflected in his behavior. These traits are permanent to the physiological makeup of the individual. Examples of some of these are: interests, temperament, sexual morality and honesty.

Personality is formed by hereditary and environmental interaction. One develops the larger portion of personality traits as a result of what is inherited from parents and grandparents. The remainder is formed by the environment—that is, the everyday encounters with friends, family, people in general, experiences, situations, circumstances, etc. the influence of parental love, standards laid down by society, endorsements or disapprovals of our decisions by friends—all play a big role in the personality cycle. As a result of such exposure our experiences will differ, our problems will differ, hence our responses will differ. This brings us to the conclusion that every human being is different.

The psychologists S. Freud maintained that personality is composed of three parts—id, ego, and superego—all interacting with one another and at the same time conflicting with one another. The id is that which we are born with; the ego and superego evolve from it. The id represents our biological and animal-like instincts—hunger, thirst, sex, aggression, etc. these operate on a "pleasure principle" and demand immediate satisfaction at any cost. The id is what most people refer to as the subconscious—something that is there that we are not aware of. The ego is an intermediary between the id and superego. It represents our learned ways of behaving and delays the satisfaction of the biological drives found in the id. In love we are human, in sexuality we are animals. Love is giving. Sex is getting (satisfaction.) the superego is the asexual product of the ego. It represents our conscience—the rules of right and wrong expressed by society and our parents.

One would think that, with the institution that lies within the personality, the individual should be morally sound and complete—especially in view of the morals and ethical standards imposed by society (as seen in the superego). However, God's righteousness transcends man's righteousness; God's standards supersede man's standards; and the old issue of sin makes that seemingly complete institution (the person) a very lacking one. Because man in his own strength cannot adhere to his own codes of standards (which are far less demanding) without failing. God says ours standards, rules and righteousness can be compared with rotten, dirty, filthy rags. So then we as Christians should be more aware of asserting the "self" (that is, ourselves) as the solution to any problem. Instead, our sure resort would be to the Christ-man in us (the Holy Spirit). When we became new creatures in Christ Jesus (2 Cor. 5:17) we were given a new nature. That is the Spirit of God which resides in us—"I will dwell in them." The secret is not so much our trying to do something or asserting our "self," but rather allowing Christ to assert His deity within us. As a further result of this, one should see an outward manifestation of His will in every situation we face. Jesus himself did *nothing* except what His Father willed and told Him to do. Everything He did was under the direction of His Father (read John 8:28). And He was God. How much more so should we be careful in seeking His will in our daily situations?

As Christians we can look into a deeper aspect of the role played by personality. The Bible plainly states that any man being in Christ is a new creature and that all (old) things are passed away. This means the whole former attitude, ways and personality should be decreased. And the residence of the Lord Jesus in the form of the Holy Spirit has now been made a part of this "new" individual. The object at this point is to yield ourselves to the leading of the Holy Spirit within us, that we may develop to be more and more like Jesus.

What was His personality? Yes, a picture of love, and all the virtues that go with it. As Paul puts it, "The life that I now live, it's not me, but Christ who is living in me." This is to say that nothing is seen of Paul as a person, but Christ dominates his life that one looking on could only see Christ living, operating and functioning in this Apostle's life. "He that hath begun a good work in you is faithful and just to continue it till the day of Christ." From the time of one's regeneration one can faithfully trust God to continue His work of saving us from SIN—SELF—and SATAN. We now have the privilege of handing over our rotten, imperfect personalities (on a daily basis) to Him and asking Him to live His holy person through us.

The saddest dilemma Christians can find themselves in is the failure to recognize their shortcomings and honestly present them to the Father. Isn't this a marvelous provision? One which stands in defiance of medical research, psychology and psychiatry, and all of the man's wisdom?

We have got to be willing to acknowledge self—that is, our attitudes, personalities, etc.—and yielding give them into His care, that by His occupancy in our place. God will be glorified by others seeing this spirit of Christ in us.

Now, you may ask what all this has to do with any relationship in marriage. The communication between two people consistently confronting one another comes to one by way of this personality of the other. That is, whatever is said takes form by how it is said, or the attitude in which it is said; and this is how the personality asserts itself. If one is almost consistent in how he or she states something (whether it be a request or otherwise), we assume that "*X*" personality or "*Y*" personality is identified with that person. Now, with the addition of love to the picture, one's personality should be completely different—that is, over and above the tolerance displayed with any other person.

It's always easy to pick out the bad points in your partner's personality and disposition and begin to destroy each other's confidence. Many couples get into a lot of trouble doing this. At the moment of contention, the first object of attack is the other's faults. Too often we can become biased in maximizing our partner's faults and minimizing our own. This can never help the situation, because a vicious cycle of retaliation has ignited and will continue to the point of anger and frustration. It doesn't require much effort to pick out the bad points. But it's always healthier to capitalize on the good ones. "It's easier to catch flies with honey than vinegar." By encouraging each other on the better points, you strengthen the communication and life-fibers in the relationship subsequently building greater love and confidence in each other.

"A word fitly spoken and in due season is like apples of gold in setting of silver."

Prov. 25:11—amplified trans.

"I'm right.... Your trouble is that.... And you're always...." It's very healthy to argue and quarrel, sometimes. Bringing things into the open with an honest approach always gets it. However, fighting fairly is important.

Any and every marriage should be specked with arguments and quarrels, provided they are constructive arguments and both parties endeavor to fight fairly. Unlike the often-stated fallacy of quarreling could be suffering emotional undernourishment, a relationship that could be dead or dying. This may stem from a lack of effective communication and understanding of each other.

In George Bach's book, *The Intimate Enemy*, he supports the approach of the pugnacious marriage. "Couples who fight together, stay together," he states. A psychologist as well as an author, Mr. Bach has authoritatively survived several thousand fights with his own wife of 28 years, and observed at least 20,000 more between his patients. One very important objective to consider in authentic anger is the fact that it brings out the truth. Mr. Bach feels that "people simply cannot release all their love feelings unless they have learned to manage their hate." And this pent-up attitude of hate must be vented before channels of radiating love are free of obstacles.

The best approach of the newly-married couple to the subject is to first realize the inevitable "oncome" of quarrels. As a result of this, agree to fight things through to a settlement—fairly. The trick here is to use words not to attack but to talk things through. To test your ability for constructive argument, try the "afterward" test: both of you feel much better; there is no lingering grievances or lasting scars; the feeling presides that something has been settled.

These are some of the tactics one should try to avoid:

- *Character Assassination*—the overall objective being to defeat the partner's ego, and in the name of honesty to do a lot of damage. An example of this is the husband who capitalizes on the wife's inability to be sexually stimulating, thereby staging an encroachment on her already unstable thoughts of her femininity.

- *Operation "Big Stick"*—quarreling to dominate the husband or wife who absolutely refuses to be the first to give in, who is willing to fight in public, or who threatens divorce. This person can often get his or her own way. When a person does this, it's often because he or she is secretly very insecure and consequently compensates with this aggressive attitude.
- *The Invited Uninvited*—soliciting an outsider's opinion in the quarrel. Positions will automatically harden, because both will try to save face instead of focusing on the issues.
- *Coward Alley*—seeking to avoid fights at any cost, or to stifle quarrels after the first few angry words.

Consistently withdrawing from fights can be one of the most unfair and frustrating tactics you can use. Suppression never works, because the damn of tolerance will give exit to a stronger current of resentment through some channel. An example of this is the wife who is blessed out for burning the husband's dinner, and sometimes without realizing it (that is the vengeance aspect) is just too tired to make love that night. Quarrels should never be killed in their prime but worked out to the point of settlement.

The use of the following pointers should aid in formulating constructive quarrel patterns: (1) First of all, you should ask yourself the questions, "Am I annoyed or really angry?" and "Do I have evidence for this?" Try to rotate methodology, using different tactics for grievances. Don't be guilty of consistently blowing steam on the same note. (2) Fight promptly to get it out of the way, thereby avoiding the rehearsed rebuttals, which will only add fire to fury. (3) Ascertain the conclusion of an argument with such questions as "Have you got it all out of your system?"

At the end of every dark night is a sunrise. After every battle are peace treaties. At the conclusion of harsh words, angry expressions, stifled fury, the dawn of flowered speech and mellowed words constitutes the final gift-wrapping on the package wherein lies renewed love and peace.

Competition

"...and thy desire shall be to thy husband."

Gen. 3:16

One of the factors most responsible for the changing attitude of the American woman is the challenge society has presented to her.

"The American woman has begun to assume a more active role in sexual behavior; her mother and grandmother assume passive postures. This reach for independence has extensive social implications. Some college-educated women feel that dependence, especially on men, is an undesirable feminine trait. They want to prove that they can function as competently and autonomously as men and this pushes them to develop academic and career skills" (Jerome Kagan).

Needless to say, this attitude has infiltrated the ranks of the average woman in our society. The effect of this disposition has incited pugnacious responses from the family head. The husband in most cases assumes a defensive position as a result of this, in defense of the cliché title he has traditionally held as the "man of the house." The arrival of a new bread-winner makes it presence felt with ensuing attitudes that may take as long as 10 years to make themselves felt. This will also give birth to a greater amount of compromise in financial and other major decisions to be made in the home.

Normal logic reveals the truth of this statement. Why shouldn't she have a 50-50 right to object if her income contributes 30%-60% of the total earning power? Let's see what Jerome Kagan continues to say in his comments.

"Why?" The intense effort spent on getting into and staying in college has persuaded the young woman that she should use her hard-won intellectual skills in a job. And technology has made it less necessary for a woman to do routine housework and forced to look outside the home for proof of her usefulness. Most human beings seek the joy of accomplishment. A man tries to gratify this need in his job, and he has something concrete with which to prove his effectiveness—an invention, a manuscript, a salary check. Woman once met her need to be useful by believing that her sweetheart, husband or children required her wisdom, skill and personal affection. Instant dinners, permissive sexual moves, and freedom for children have undermined this role. It is too early to predict the effect of this female unrest. It should lead to a more egalitarian relation between the sexes. *It could make each partner so reluctant to submerge his individual autonomy, and admit his need for the other, that each walks a lonely and emotionally insulated path.* Let's hope it does not."* From Psychology Today Magazine, July 1969. Copyright Communications Research Machines, Inc.

He has not said a lot in these two paragraphs. Looking a little further into this new direction of woman's autonomy, it says enough to demand our attention. We can save ourselves in a little time in referring to any number of authorities in the gamut by going to the zenith of authorities, the Bible.

Nowhere in the Bible will you find a statement compelling a wife to love her husband. However, on more than one occasion the Scripture points out the husband's duty to love the wife. The requirement imposed on the wife is that she honor the husband in obedience. This is not to say that she shouldn't love her husband. Taking into consideration Mr. Kagan's views, we can hardly conceive of this disposition under our present social structure. So what if a woman contributes to the income of the family? Does this give her the right to supersede the passive role Scripture has maintained for her? It's all really very simple. God's word doesn't change. The pattern of her behavior has been formulated and outlined to be followed.

I spoke to a young lady once who related the story of her salvation experience, which was met with total scorn and indifference by her husband. At first there was an intensified effort to get him "saved." The opposition that she faced as a result of this caused her feelings for him to wane—so much so that after a short period of time she actually began to hate and detest him.

One day during this time, the Lord brought her to a point of pensive spiritual exploration where she began to realize her subordinate role, in which she should be submissive to the desires of her husband rather than selfishly seeking to be satisfied in her own desires. Her journey through the "Word" had its inception in Genesis Chapter 3.

Too many sisters today fail to appreciate the literal interpretation of this verse, which is carried over in the New Testament to 1 Peter 3:5 and 6. Many female believers like to think that the change of norms and ways of thinking in our time merits the equivalent change of God's design for our family structure. Much to the contrary, this may prove to be very disappointing. God's word is the same yesterday, today and forever. Before His word will change, heaven and earth will pass away. (Matt. 24:35)

Getting back to the story, this young sister began to re-evaluate her attitude towards her husband, who at this time was contemptible in her sight (to the point of her actually hating him). Retracing these attitudes, she found that in desiring what she wanted she usually ended up frustrated and unsatisfied, one reason being that she maintained a high degree or expectancy. She set to work immediately in correcting this—"her desire to be to her husband"—and found that by giving of herself and seeking to satisfy the comforts of her husband, she was more than able to feel the rewards of passion in the response of her husband to the new phase of unselfish appeasement. By giving, she got.

Her attitude towards her husband changed from disdain to delight. In a matter of weeks the cycle of retaliation and frustration was transformed to reconciliation and jubilation—outcome of simply following God's established design.

Both husband and wife have the responsibility of seeking the other's interest first. As human beings we sometimes uniquely complicate things by seeking to satisfy "self;" or helping God not to show us what we should do; or even better yet, not seeking to know what His will for us in "that" situation entails.

The cost of leadership for the husband is a dear one. Too often the husband wants the God-given leadership position and assumes only the title and not the function. Leadership is the sacrificing of one's self void of any self-interest, motivated by all intentions for the good and nourishment of the body (wife and family)—and, in the case of Christians, for the primary goal of God's glory.

Sometimes the husband takes advantage of his leadership position by seeking to attain his own ends, and consequently loses the respect and/or trust of his dear ones in the finale. Much wisdom is required here on the part of the husband. Embarrassment should never be felt in praying for this wisdom to pilot a family through the seas of everyday life.

"Likewise, ye husbands dwell with them according to knowledge, giving honor unto the wife us unto the weaker vessel" (1 Pet. 3:7). The husband, here depicted as the stronger vessel, is exhorted to exercise special care to the wife as the weaker vessel. The premium on this directive is so high that to fail automatically short-circuits your communication with the Father (v. 7).

Male dominance in family matters was an Eve hand-me-down hang-up. Genesis 3:16 relates the story as it was and the consequences as they now stand. "unto the woman he said, I will greatly multiply thy sorrow and thy conception; in sorrow thou shalt bring forth children; and thy desire shall be to thy husband, and he shall rule over thee." Social norms cannot change this. History has mirrored the results of countless numbers of cultures which have risen and fallen, each with their adopted family norms and mores. The foundations of truth in God's word are not affected by man's changing standards. His word is the same yesterday, today and forever. Women, regardless of educational, financial, or any other assets are instructed to maintain a passive role.

A wife (or prospective wife) must be game to see herself as a leader, willing to be led—a leader in comforting the needs of the family. Gen 24:63-67 reflects a beautiful picture of this. Isaac meets his bride-to-be for the first time and experiences love at first sight. The setting is ravishing. Isaac is in the field near sunset meditating (taking care if God's business) when out of the east comes a cloud of dust which moment by moment reveals the return of the servant who was commissioned to salvage a wife for Isaac. As they come closer and closer, the excitement within Isaac becomes unbearable. At this point he glimpses the beauty of the feminine form that is seated on the camel in the distance, and runes to meet her.

The Bible further goes on to tell us in v. 67that Isaac's mother died shortly after she met his bride. But in the midst of the calamity, Rebekah reflected *life* in emanating warm consolation. You would have to examine the close relationship of a mother to an only son to appreciate how meaningful the comfort of a concerned and loving wife is in a relationship. "And Isaac was comforted after his mother's death." Rebekah was that comfort the Scriptures refer to here.

Her leadership does not end here. The wife is a leader in the maintenance of family unity; a leader maintenance of the home; a leader in securing the affections of the family—recognizing her value, and at the same time willing to be led by her husband.

Chapter IV
Marriage
[ADDENDUM]

Jerome Kagan's statement in Psychology Today magazine, July 1969, "It is too early to predict the effects of this female unrest. It should lead to more equalitarian relations between the sexes. It could make each partner so reluctant to submerge as individual or autonomy, and admit its need for the other, that each walks a lonely and emotional insulated path. Let's hope it does not." Now after 50 years we have solid empirical results.

The story is told of an old itinerant preacher who was passing through a town on a Sunday afternoon and stopped by a church where he observed a woman preaching. After the service he stood up and began scolding the woman for preaching based on 1 Corinthians 14:34. The woman responded in a huff, where would you men be today without us women? He replied very gently, sister, we would have been in the Garden of Eden. So much for wishful thinking "smile". On to reality. So why can't God be female? On entering New York Theological Seminary, these are questions I was hearing in discussion groups. The new curriculum which included Feminist Theology would have all the answers. Coming out of a "fundamentalist" society I was in shock. The basics in Feminist Theology is that God is in fact female. Front and centers the major issue of **male dominance** in the Christian marriage. Time and space will not allow us the luxury of exploring their ideology which would take up two semesters. Feminist Theology is diametrically opposed to Fundamentalism. Fundamentalism evolved as a consensus among the main line protestant groups (to include the brethren) around 1910 to 1920. They espoused these 5 basic fundamentals: the infallibility of the scriptures; virgin birth of Jesus; Christ's death was the atonement for sin; bodily resurrection of Jesus; and the reality of the miracles of Jesus the infallibility of scripture lends itself to strict literalism taking God's Word literally also known as biblical literalism.

Feminist Refute

Genesis 3:16, "*Unto the woman he said, I will greatly multiply thy sorrow in thy conception; in sorrow thou shalt bring forth children; and by desire shall be to thy husband, and he shall rule over thee.*"

Ephesians 5:22-24, "*Wives, submit yourself unto your own husbands as unto the Lord. For the husband is the head of the wife, even as Christ is the head of the church; and He is the savior of the body. Therefore as the church is subject unto Christ, so let the wives be to their own husbands in everything.*"

1 Peter3:1, "*In the same manner, ye wives be in subjection to your own husbands, that if any obey not the Word, they also may without the Word be won by the behavior of the wives.*"

1 Corinthians 11:7-9, "*For a man indeed ought not to cover his head, for as much as he is the <u>image and glory of God</u>; but the woman is the glory of man. Fr the man is not of the woman, but the woman is of the man. Neither was the man created for the woman, but the woman for the man.*"

Man is the glory of God. Man is the glory of God. Man is the glory of God. Woman **<u>is not</u>** the glory of God. Woman is the glory of man. Before Eve was created, God gave man His glory, dominion over every living thing. This did not include Eve until her disobedience—the fall. Here is the problem. Man is created, conceived and wired from birth with this "dominion" paradigm; given by his creator. Man does not understand this mindset in his subconscious. He experiences this as instinct. He doesn't know why he feels this way and can't explain it. Example the female police officer, judge, or CEO exercises authority and the initial response from men may be resentment/opposition. Societal norms, education, etc. conditions males to accept this female dominance/authority we are not dealing with right or wrong, just understanding feelings. We live in the world, but God's rules are regulated to the church community.

Let me introduce a personal example of how real this struggle, battle, and war is. I have a personal and dear friend who retired a professional in her field. She exercised a lot of authority in her daily Modus Operandi on her job. Many of her subordinates were males she was amazed at the many times her orders were flagrantly ignored by males, sometimes at the risk of their jobs. On her home front she had problems grappling with suggestions and orders from her husband. Sister M is a devout and loving Christian. I've known her for over 40 years. To date she is the holiest female I know. A major problem was that her salary was double what her husband earned and she struggled with having to obey him. God did convict her 3 years into her marriage of how important obedience was. She admitted to me how much of a relief this was to her emotionally when she accepted it as God's will. Sister M has now been a widow for over 30 years. I shared with her my thoughts of doing this sequel. When I mentioned my thoughts on woman's liberation and the subject of the Christian wife's role, a long discussion ensued. She bristled at the words "male dominance". It took a lot of explaining and historical concept to see God's mandate on the subject. She joins millions in the initial reaction to the words, idea or engagement of the phenomenon of male dominance. The flesh is a powerful reactant. Yes the chemical reaction of the "flesh" reared its ugly head. The pride, that's part of the "flesh", refuses to accept this. The battle goes on.

Christian's are bound to the Word of God which clearly states Deuteronomy 4:2, "*Ye shall not add unto the Word which I command you neither shall ye diminish aught from it that ye may keep the commandments of the Lord your God which I command you*". Deuteronomy 12:32, "*What things soever I command you, observe to do it: thou shall not add there to nor diminish from it.*" Jesus as the living Word proclaims I am the same yesterday today and forever (Hebrews 13:8). In other words, nothing in my Word changes. He has left us the written Word—the Bible. Therefore there is no rationale, interpretation or justification for any guidance outside of the Word of God. God's Word is universal and timeless. 1 Samuel 15:22, "Behold, to obey is better than sacrifice, and to hearken in the fat of rams." Studies show that this type of Old Testament worship was the ultimate outreach to God. So. God was/is saying your obedience to Me is far more important than your sacrifices to me. All our praying, fasting, preaching, teaching, service, tithing, church attendance, mean nothing to God if we don't obey Him/His Word.

How would you feel if you knew you were confronting the glory of God? That the glory of God was actually in your presence? Would you honor it? Would you respect it? Would you reverence it? Or would you spit on it? Or desecrate it? Man is the glory of God. Your husband is the glory of God. God says, "*Wives, submit yourself unto your own husband, as unto the Lord,*" (Ephesians 5:22-24). Jesus in another example of transposing into first person "*...As much as you've done this to the least of my brethren, you've done it unto me,*" (Matthew 25:40). Yes, this man with all his faults, defects and shortcomings; is the glory of God. Do you want to see him change? Then you first have to change. If you don't want God's will for your life and your marriage, you can stop here. Otherwise, your first step is to sit down with him; equipped with this new knowledge, and apologize for your attitude and actions over the months/years. For not acknowledging his leadership (try to be specific if you can). "Can you forgive me and accept my apologies? Going forward, I won't be perfect but with God's help I'm all in to enjoy our life together". And just do it!!! After his initial shock period you will see a major change in him in the weeks and months that follow. "...She that is married, careth for the things of the world, how she may please her husband," 1 Corinthians 7:34.

It is logical that Feminist Theology comes out of Feminist Intellectualism and the women's liberation movement. Many good things came out of the women's liberation movement. It changed how women were perceived in their cultures, redefined the socio-economic and political roles of women in society and transformed mainstream society. On the other side of this world's system it ravaged and devastated the church body from pulpit to pew. To answer Jerome Kagan's question of 1969, the divorce rates were off the charts as a result of this new ideology and fabricated freedom. It fractured the institution of marriage in the church. This spirit of rebellion was pervasive throughout the late 60s into the 80s. Even in the ghetto/inner cities, one could hear the classic refrain, "I can be poor by myself." Thereby justifying resisting male assertions of authority in a marriage relationship.

It was during this era I had graduated from Pennsylvania medical college in a pharmaceutical specialty to instruct physicians under the umbrella of Smith Kline and French. Looking back, this was the greatest vocation I obtained in my work history at that time. I was responsible for mentoring over 300 physicians in my territory. The best memory I had was my parents telling me that their family doctor had given me title of being the doctor's doctor. At his request I had gone outside my territory to update him on a major medical breakthrough which would eliminate a need for surgery. What I had discovered in my comradery with this medical community was that there was a high rate of divorce among doctors. At that time as much as 38% of the medical community i.e. doctors and nurses as couples in my area were from the Asian peninsula (India and all Asia). In those respective countries/cultures, a woman's submissive role was a given. By coming to America the experience of liberty and freedom ignited this new pervasive awareness, compounding the air of independence. The consequences for these actions were multilateral. I have a female friend who has been a dynamic seasoned and charismatic preacher for years. She married to the first over the age of 40, she had a strong personality. I asked her, what did you say when the minister came to "obey him?" She responded, "Wes. I paused for the longest time and finally caught myself and said yes." They did start a church with him as pastor and her as assistant pastor and are doing well.

I was recently surprised to find one of the greatest and most successful female evangelist in our time ran a series about her struggle with yielding to male/husband authority in both the marriage relationship and in general. There's no question about Joyce Meyer's success in reaching millions for the expansion and nursing of God's kingdom. And yet, in her greatness she struggles to keep down this enemy, THE FLESH. As a reminder, the 3 enemies of the born again believer are: the world, the flesh, and the devil (see Appendix 3). You can go to YouTube search and request Joyce Meyers, "The Married Woman's Struggle With Submission" and "Rebellious Wives Who Refuse To Submit 4/17". Share these must see videos. I think of how many thousands of marriages that could have been saved hearing this powerful testimony and information. Both Sister M and Joyce have given us a clear understanding of the problem. We have to put into perspective that man is born in sin and shaped in iniquity (Psalm 51:5) we are all born with a sinful nature. The Bible calls it the FLESH. This flesh is in rebellion against the Spirit also created in us. As you may recall we are a tri-part entity Spirit Soul Body. Our Spirit, is the god consciousness within us our rebellion resides within the soul/mind that demands its own desires and satisfaction. Without the influence of the Spirit we lose. Flesh, "Refers not only to the body but also the soul/mind that **<u>is not</u>** brought under subjection to our Spirit." So rebellion over authority, in this case male authority is natural and part of our DNA. This can only be countered by the "will" (that resides in the soul), volunteering obedience to the Word of God through our Spirit. Voluntary subordination to our Spirit—choice!!!

1 Timothy 2:12, "*But I permit not a woman to teach, nor usurp authority over the man...*" A noticeable exception is found in Acts 18:24-26. Here Aquila and Priscilla veterans of the faith, hear for the first time this superbly eloquent brother preaching on a novice level. Recognizing his gift they humbly take him aside and expound the kingdom in great depth for the glory of God. Usurp is the key hear, the word usurp is the key here. Webster defines usurp as follows: to size or exercise authority or possession wrongfully. There's no question of the abilities in the dynamic contributions of the female cleric both now and down through the ages. It is my opinion based on scripture that she can pastor or preach as long as she chooses the humility of being under her husband or bishop/church leader. He is her umbrella and she is therefore sanctified/covered by his authority. Therefore she **<u>is not</u>** usurping authority. This is a similar concept we find in 1 Corinthians 7:12-16 which reads as follows, "*...If any brother has a wife that believeth not, and she be pleased to dwell with him, let him not put her away...the unbelieving wife is sanctified by the husband... how knowest thou old man, whether thou shalt save thy wife?*"

In conclusion of this subject matter of male dominance I will share a scripture I had promulgated with pastors in my ministry of "helps" (1 Corinthians 12:28) in the body of Christ for over

40 years. A scripture that has been greatly overlooked and discounted. 1 Peter 3:1, "*In the same manner ye wives be in subjection to your own husbands that, if any obey not the Word they also may without the Word be won by the conversation/behavior/conduct of the wives…*" I've heard a couple of megachurch pastors applauding the classic case of the wife who's told not to go to church by an "unsaved" husband who defiantly disobeys him and goes anyway with the encouragement of the pastor. WRONG!!! In this powerful passage God takes a back seat!!! Just think, God the almighty, the all-powerful elevating the wife to a higher position than Himself; to say without my Word…your behavior to this unsaved man is more powerful and persuasive, "*For the preaching of the cross is to them that perish foolishness,*" (1 Corinthians 1:18). Here is your opportunity to flesh out all of the dynamics of true Christianity and obedience to God's Word. There's nothing more powerful than the Word of God on this planet. We know that Jesus was the living Word and left us with his written Word-the Bible (John 1). Wife, equipped with this knowledge you have an awesome responsibility.

On the subject of behavior, wife, is God's Word true to you? Proverbs 15:1, "*A soft word turneth away wrath/anger…*" Simple compliance to a husband's request with a soft and verbal affirmation defuses any argument or turmoil. Does this mean that you agree with him? Maybe not. But equally important here is to express **your** view of the situation and assertion that your obedience to God's Word is of great importance in your marriage and your love for him (your husband) is what you hold dear and ask, "What do you think of my view/feelings in this situation?"

Proverbs 15:1, "*A soft answer turneth away wrath, but grievous words stir up anger.*" Can there be any softer answer than the Word of God? By a spiritual osmosis, i.e. allowing the Word of God to become part of us, and speaking through us will result in that soft answer. Countless times in my experience where I dealt with an angry situation I was often amazed at the calm that came out of my mouth. On reflection, I was always amused, that wasn't me. I know what I would've said. With years of practicing wanting what God wants, the Holy spirit within reconstructs the attitude demeanor and words that come. As a wife to that UNSAVED husband that soft answer can be reinforced by: 1 Corinthians 13:7-8, "*Love beareth all things, believeth all things, hopeth all things, endureth all things. Love never faileth;*" Let this soft answer from God minister to you. Now with God's help, the Holy Spirit within you, you can engage the situation, passing on that soft answer.

2 Timothy 2-3, "Thou therefore endure hardness, as a good soldier of Jesus Christ." As male and female, we are called upon by God to be good soldiers. I can tell you as a veteran, that the first duty of a soldier is to obey-obedience. Without this, there would be chaos confusion and consumption. This would be a house divided against itself. While enduring hardness on any level in our Christian walk we can take solace in 1 Corinthians 10:31and Colossians 3:17, "*Whatever ye do, do all to the glory of God.*" "*Whatever you do in word or deed, do all in the name of the Lord Jesus.*" As soldiers in God's army this is our commission and letting our lights. Shine. For the SAVED husband, a different story. You won't agree on everything. If you did, one of you wouldn't be necessary. The obligation of obedience on the part of the wife

still stands. The husband has the obligation of "knowing" and "pleasing" his wife (1 Corinthians 7:33, 1 Peter 3:7). So a discussion on the issue is in order. This is a major part of learning each other as you become one.

The Bible says on two accounts there has never been a wiser man than Solomon on the Earth. Yet all his wisdom came to nothing because of his compliance to the behavior/conduct of his pagan wives. **A woman's behavior/conduct is incredibly powerful**. The oxymoron here is that she, in reality dominates the marriage relationship when she complies in an attitude of obedience to the Word and her husband. To the saved "husband" give one hundred percent to learning her and accommodating her. Otherwise your prayers go nowhere. At least, not very far. That's power!!! Wife power. In the scenario of the defiant wife and unsaved husband, the correct response should be as follows: "The Word of God tells me to obey you, and if that's what you want, I will obey your request." Then continue to witness to him. Pray in earnest for God to change his mind and heart. God will do it, if you remain consistent. Reach out to prayer warriors in your circle, a breakthrough is on the way. Isn't it amazing that in God's chain of command He upholds even the unsaved husband as the authority over the wife? Wow...ultimately her behavior will carry the day and preserve that home. This is why her price is far beyond rubies, which is more precious than gold (Proverbs 31:10). This is not only for their happiness but God's glory. It is supposed to reflect the relationship of Jesus to His church. The world is watching.

CHAPTER V
SEX

"The wife does not have authority over her own body, but the husband does; and likewise also the husband does not have authority over his own body, but the wife does. Stop depriving one another, except by agreement for a time that you may devote yourselves to prayer, and come together again lest Satan tempt your because of your lack of self-control."

I Cor. 7:4-5.

In the case of most mammals there is a marked period of time in which the female is in heat and seeks sexual satisfaction. This period is known as "estrus." Let's look at one example of this—the rat. During the period of ovulation, for about 19 hour every 4 or 5 days of the female rat is in estrus. During this time both the male and the female pay a great deal of attention to each other. Normally, they do not; because rats, like most mammals, mate only when the female is in heat and fertilization can take place.

Unlike her female mammal cousin, the human female alone among mammals has no easily-identifiable period of estrus, taking into consideration that human sexual relations take place for a variety of non-reproductive reasons. This is not totally foreign in the sexual behavior of the remaining mammal class. Apes and monkeys sometimes mate when the female is not in estrus, although neither appears to enjoy sex as much under those conditions.

The absence of estrus in the human family thus places a higher demand on the male to promote sexual satisfaction year-round.

Sometimes either spouse will use sexual deprivation as a tool of retaliation, especially in the case of an annoyed wife. This is not only cruel but can become mentally torturing. The Apostle commands us (by the inspiration of God, the Holy Spirit), not to do this. One very deceptive way of getting out of this is to volunteer our bodies, and yet deny our partner our total self. This is physical involvement without an emotional investment. Sexual intercourse void of a total pouring out of one's self (the affectionate and whole-hearted effort of wanting to please your partner) is another way of saying "sex without satisfaction." If there is satisfaction under those conditions, it will eventually be short-lived.

"Husbands dwell with them according to knowledge" (1 Pet. 3:7). This simply puts a highly significant responsibility on the husband to study the needs of his wife, the things that please her. What makes her happy? What makes her feel loved? What pleases her sexually? What annoys or disgusts her? What turns her on? Learning every facet of her personality is the way to know what pleases her *in toto*. This, of course, takes time and isn't done in two or three.

"Women are hard to understand," it is always said. One reason for this is the fact that a woman doesn't usually think in terms of logic, particularly in a depressive or frustrated mood. One of the unique traits that distinguishes the female from the male is the fact that under these conditions she is usually inclined to think with her emotions.

A husband should be particularly concerned with this factor. A woman cannot be treated as a man, inasmuch as her emotional reaction is literally that of a comparatively sensitive nature. These reactions or actions have nothing to do with intelligence or logical thinking; they are totally divorced. This is why the Word of God so emphatically gets across the point of the husband catering to the wife and extending understanding patience. Her emotional network is necessary to penetrate and appease, and this can only be done effectively with love and patience. The active function of this aspect of love is only a part of studying her needs.

Let's focus our attention on the sexual needs of the wife. How does she like to be loved? What new methods of stimulation and approaches have you both tried together? The husband's labor in this area of exploring is very essential. It is necessary for him to study all the methods and formulas that may lead to the satisfaction and pleasure of the wife. There is no room for formality or scorn in love-making. Nothing is too despicable to try in all your experimentations.

The Sex Act

One of the saddest mistakes made in pursuing the sexual endeavor is for the participants (especially the husband) to think that sexual satisfaction for both parties begins in the bedroom. Medical authorities confirm the existence of sexual problems in ½ to ¾ of all married couples, and for this reason our attention to this matter cannot be over-emphasized. Let us take into consideration the fact that medical and psychological hang-ups can exist. These will not be discussed. Our spotlight is on the normal couple.

The end product of enjoyed sex is mutual satisfaction. If sex becomes anything but "enjoyed sex," it is only physical sexual involvement. This means that both parties are involved physically in the act, but both parties are involved physically in the act, but both will not achieve mutual satisfaction. The male partner is almost always a recipient of sexual satisfaction, so we will focus most of our attention on the satisfaction of the female.

She is not merely a satisfaction-post for your sexual needs. You hold the keys to "turn her on." This feat should be pursued with all diligence and thoughtfulness. Kissing and petting should be the physical genesis of every sexual intercourse. The caressing and kissing of the breast, the stroking of the thighs by the fingers, the kissing of the neck, thighs, etc., are all part of this process.

Before we go into the actual pros on the stimulation of the wife, let's consider possible hindrances to this mission. The sexual appeasement of the wife does not start in the bedroom. Let's see why.

Too often the objective of stimulating sexual satisfaction of the female has been thought to begin with sex-play moments prior to intercourse. However, there's more to all of this than that. The husband (if you're not already aware of it) knows that the little things—which add up—make the big difference. "Sex enjoyed" by husband and wife is perhaps the highest level of physical appeasement that can be experienced.

The time you've spent not responding to the simple requests for a glass of water in the middle of the night; perhaps going out to get a favorite treat on a cold's winter night; the negative attitude when asked to help—all these are some of many seemingly-small factors which help to structure hidden dissension. Yes, by your going the extra miles, a woman feels loved and cared for. True, these are all simple things; but to a woman they make a big difference. Suppose we were to multiply all of these little unfulfilled requests (which produce dissatisfaction) times the amount of times per week they went unsatisfied, then multiply the months or perhaps years. Wouldn't this be a disaster to a woman's ego? The critical disaster here is that the attitude which is created by the wife as a result of the husband's despondency multiples with an equal amount of frustration and contempt. It's only a question of time before the cement in this type of relationship hardens, and you have a perfectly solid foundation of chaos. The deceptive fact about this is that it doesn't usually come to the surface immediately. It may take several months, and as long as several years.

The dissatisfaction of the wife now becomes so routine that it becomes a part of the family's everyday life. Neither him nor she is aware that these problems have stemmed from these little matters, which grown out of proportion. When you add all of these little things up they comprise enough weight to think about. The fulfillment of these little requests not only sets the stage for being "cared for," but it makes her that much more eager to create satisfaction for her husband—this, by virtue of her satisfaction. The formula we discussed in the earlier chapters is essential to the application here.

Now, with these little things established, nothing hinders a free and receptive mind for being "petted." Her attitude and frame of mind are free from dissatisfactions and frustrations. Hence, she is free to give herself over to your advances.

The amount of time spent in this is a unique and exclusive formula which can only be worked out between the involved parties. Particular attention should be given to how much stimulation is needed to bring her to a point of considerable reaction. During this stage of stimulation, "petting" should conclude with the manipulation of the genital area, penetrating the inner depths of the vagina to the point of stroking the clitoris. This is a highly sensitive organ which requires knowledge of its location, as well as working-knowledge of manipulating it. (I recommend a medical guide to find its location).

To every sexual endeavòr for satisfaction, there is the necessary requirement of sexual adjustment to contend with. Nevertheless, this is an investment which will lend air to high dividends and returns in hours of happiness. Like everything else that is truly worth something, this comes at a high price.

At this point we can journey into stage two—that is, the actual genital contact, or sexual intercourse. The entrance of the penis into the vagina should be accomplished with the objective of achieving orgasm (sexual appeasement for both).

"Climax" is a word that can be used interchangeably with the word "orgasm." This is the ultimate fulfillment of the nerve sensations that commenced with the excitation of the sexual organs.

Now, with the entrance of the penis into the vagina established, we can concentrate our attention on the body movement. The rhythm of breathing and the pelvic thrust should be synchronized. The forward thrust of the pelvis should coincide with the exhalation of breath. This does not exclude the wife from moving during the interchange.

Many women have felt that, by moving during sexual intercourse, this reflects an open intent for pleasure. This, of course, to them is not only embarrassing but equally uncouth. To be in this frame of mind is to be in chains of slavery. To be aware of restricting the body's natural reaction to this sensation will automatically hinder the natural feeling of giving one's entire self. As a result, the female does not receive complete orgasm. Even if she does reach a climax, it's only partial.

If we look at the other side of the pendulum we see mass-movement response from the female as a false façade of satisfaction. That is, she does this body movement and responds only in motion void of real stimulation. This is not only deceptive but also injurious to the relationship. Can you imagine a man being disillusioned by his wife into thinking he is satisfying her, only to perhaps find out in the long run that this was absolutely false? Think of all that wasted time in maladjustment towards each other! The husband would do better flogging a dead horse if expecting a response. During this period, he was adjusting to a pattern of movement and timing which was not parallel to the real sexual needs and satisfaction of the wife. Had there been an honest admittance of these things initially, many therapies could have been pursued, and satisfaction for both would not only have been forthcoming but equally rewarding.

The climax of this involvement for the male is almost always satisfaction. This comes in two phases: (1) convulsive reaction of the whole body; (2) ejaculation (release of sperm from the male organ). On the other hand, the climax of this involvement for the female is one of three: (1) convulsive reactions of the whole body; (2) contraction of muscle on the surrounding vagina muscle. Both of these are reflected in female orgasm. The third is most unwanted: frustration (incomplete satisfaction). This does not mean total failure on the part of the make. One of the elementary facts of sexual development of sexual desire found in the male, as compared to the retarded pace of the female. Even with the most skilled advances of an adept husband, no guarantee of the wife's sexual satisfaction is forthcoming.

The reason for this could be one of many. Some women experience a climax only after being married for some time. Some do so only occasionally, which may be attributed to a cyclical nature reaching a peak before, during, or after the menstrual period. Other reasons could be mood and temperament, as was discussed in the earlier part of the chapter; medical or psychological hang-ups; or lack of proper sexual adjustment (this is to include proper timing). A momentary failure to prompt a sexual climax in the wife is not a total failure. Remember, this has to be worked at. Anything of true value comes at a dear cost. In this case, consistent, sincere investigation and experimentation will fill the bill.

One of the chief shortcomings on the part of the husband promoting orgasm for the wife is what is termed as "premature ejaculation." This is when the husband climaxes before the wife does. Frustration is felt particularly in the wife. If this happens consistently, it can become almost equally frustration to the concerned husband. Sexual adjustment is usually focused around this-up. If, in following the prescribed methods mentioned in the former part of this chapter, you consistently encounter this problem, try sitting down with each other and honestly discussing it. One of the most essential ingredients in sexual adjustment is honest and straightforward communication with each other, jointly seeking to strike a light in the darkness. Talk it over and—"try, try again."

This therapy cannot be overemphasized. Talking it over after the sexual involvement, if done in earnest, will set the proper frame of mind, after which it should be rewarding to try again.

This conclusion may seem a bit ironical to you, but no man can satisfy a woman or give her an orgasm. He can only create the conditions that make possible her self-fulfillment, but the rest is up to her. She need not be as excited as the man to get initial as well as final satisfaction, but she must consciously want to engage in the act for her own pleasure and satisfaction.

Many sexologists recommend that the husband and wife caress each other in the genital area, particularly in the case of newly-weds on the first night. This enables the new wife to actually see and understand the relationship of friction versus contact of the nerves in the head of the male organ. This should also be the ideal time for the husband to discover the location of the clitoris and at the same time commence experimental manipulation of it, to the taste and enjoyment of the wife (she should at this point direct him according to the height of her sensation).

What if your wife does not have this strong desire for sex—particularly in the case of the average man? Do you continue to negotiate sexual involvement? Psychiatric tests have proven that it is far better to allow a woman in this state to determine the course of sexual activity, and to avoid any participation in the sex act itself until some desire is felt. She should be allowed to act in accordance with her feelings. Psychiatric experience shows that once the woman begins to assert this right, it is not long before positive sexual feelings arise. In simple summary, she has got to want to. If you continue otherwise, you can almost be guaranteed a married life weeded with sexual disaster.

Psychiatrists distinguish between a "clitoral orgasm" and a "Vaginal orgasm." "Clitoral orgasm" is the fondling of the clitoris to the point of climax. This is usually pursued in one of two way—when the female masturbates, or when the male initiates this action. Sex authorities recognize this is a release of partial satisfaction rather than a complete orgasm. Vaginal orgasm, on the other hand, is achieved in the inner depths of the vagina—a journey to be made if the female experiences a climax. It should come as no surprise that this resulting complete satisfaction is fulfilled only by the union of these two body-instruments which God has endorsed in his wonderful creation of organic structure and purpose.

It is here in these hours of experimentation and the pursuit of happiness, that we can see the beautiful role of love and sex entwined to climax into stronger love, greater happiness, and warmer appreciation for each other. Sex was meant to be beautiful clean, lovely, and even holy.

Chapter V
Sex Part II
[ADDENDUM]

Libido is a person's overall sexual drive or desire for sexual activity. Libido is influenced by biological, psychological and social factors. Sex hormones such as testosterone and estrogen regulate libido in humans. Primarily testosterone in males and some in females and estrogen in women. The testosterone in females is produced by the ovaries in small amounts. Combined with estrogen the female testosterone helps with the growth, maintenance and repair of a woman's reproductive tissues, bone mass and human behavior. Testosterone is mainly produced in men by the testicles. It affects the man's appearance and sexual development. It stimulates sperm production as well as a man's sex drive, components of testosterone are aggression and competition. Testosterone levels determine the level of sexual interest. For the sake of our discussion we will look at three levels of testosterone: low-level testosterone, average-level testosterone, and high-level testosterone. Multiple studies have shown men who are high-level are more likely to engage in extramarital sex. One study had shown a direct correlation between high-level testosterone and dominance, especially among the most violent criminals in prison.

High-level testosterone is highly desirable in the area of competition. Pick any sport. Here is where society accepts this abnormality. The transferring of this sexual energy is referred to as sublimation. I think it's fair to say all champions, male or female, have high-level testosterone. On the sexual end, sometimes it gets them in trouble. We have to recognize an important narrative here introduced by Hoebel, who after extensive research and tests concluded that "Man is born with polygamous proclivities."

Michael Jordan was married for over 16 years before his wife suspected the alleged dozens of affairs leading to divorce. Wilt Chamberlain played it safe and stayed single knowing his appetite for several hundred women a year was his norm. Among modern history United States Presidents I can think of no more trusting and moving dedication for husband and wife fidelity than Harry S. Truman and his wife Elizabeth. Yet by stark contrast his successor Dwight D. Eisenhower had Kay in the background of his marriage. This was common knowledge to his inner circle. This phenomenon, i.e. Hoebel's assertion, has existed with Presidents, high-profile sports and entertainment figures as well as the average everyday man since time began. There has not been a year since President Truman (1950s) where a high-profile divorce or proceeding hasn't surfaced as a result of this phenomenon. We will review some biblical examples further on in the chapter. But first, some basics. Fertility is one of the major differences between men and women. On one hand, men are continuously fertile from puberty to a hundred years of age even though by that time they are physically unable to engage in sexual activities. Their sperms are still viable but poor in quality. Men are fertile this long because there is a continuous production of sperms through the process called spermatogenesis.

Women on the other hand are fertile for 12 hours each month from menarche up until they are in their 50s, when menopause begins for most women. Fertility for them are limited because they have a set number of eggs. At this stage sexual changes are imminent. Vaginal dryness and a loss of sex drive is common. Usually sex is not enjoyed as much and reaching orgasms become more difficult. As long as it isn't painful regular sexual activity may help keep the vagina healthy by promoting blood flow. In this stage of menopause ovaries have stopped sending out the required number of eggs to allow pregnancy. However, in every generation a miracle baby happens. As far as diminished sex drive at this stage, there are always exceptions to every rule. In my private practice I had seen three women, two in their 80s and one in their 90s, that were sexually active with their respective husbands.

Birds do it, bees do it, and men do it any old time. But women will only do it if the candles are scented just right—and their partner has done the dishes first. A stereotype, sure, but is it true? Do men really have stronger sex drives than women? Well, yes, they do. Study after study shows that men's sex drives are not only stronger than women's, but much more straightforward the sources of women's libido, by contrast are much harder to pin down. It's common wisdom that women place more value on emotional connection as a spark of sexual desire. But women also appear to be heavily influenced by social and cultural factors as well. According to Edwin O. Laumann, Ph.D., a professor of Sociology at the University of Chicago, the majority of adult men under 60 think about sex at least once a day. Only 4 of women say that they think about it that frequently. As men and women age, each fantasizes less, but men still fantasize twice as often.

In a survey of studies comparing male and female sex drives, Roy Baumeister, a social psychologist at Florida State University, found that men reported more spontaneous sexual arousal and had more frequent and varied fantasies. He concludes after several surveys men want sex more often than women. At the start of a relationship, in the middle of it, and after many years of it. Men, on average, take four minutes from the point of entry till ejaculation, according to Laumann. Women usually take around 10 to 11 minutes to reach orgasm—if they do. That's another difference between the sexes—how often they have an orgasm during sex. Among men who are a part of a couple, 75% say they always have an orgasm as opposed to 26% of the women. So much for basics.

It had to be one of the most glorious days in the history of Israel. If Pay Per View was available the entire population would be sitting at the edge of their seats. In the arena were two armies. The army of the Philistines and the army of Israel. The unmistakable presence of an 8-ft-plus giant captures the immediate attention of all spectators. Here was David and Goliath. The greatest upset in the history of one on one combat had taken place. We have to step back here and recognize that this teenage marvel was anointed king a few weeks earlier. 1 Samuel 16:13: "Then Samuel took the horn of oil and anointed him the Spirit of the Lord came upon David from that day onward...." But even prior to this we read in verse 18: "I have seen a son of Jesse...a mighty valiant man, and a man of war...." David had a reputation.

Killing both a lion and a bear while defending his father's sheep didn't go unnoticed. His natural strength, now armed with the presence of God's Holy Spirit, gave him unparalleled power. It's no wonder the stone actually sunk into the skull of Goliath (1 Samuel 17:49). He would become the greatest King in Israel and Judah's 210-year history. I consider this remarkable taking into account the roll call of dozens of kings that reigned in that period. This was not an accident. David, even as a child, had a heart that sought after God. God, who measures the heart recognized this and does something spectacular and unprecedented. David becomes the first and only King to be given God's Holy Spirit (1 Samuel 16:13).

He was very aware of this privilege in adulthood and we find him begging God not to take it back in Psalms 51. Here we recognize God's mercy in human failure. It would be over a thousand years before humanity would be blessed with this greatest of all gifts which would lead to eternal life conditionally. This is the promise Jesus gave us after his resurrection from the grave. His Holy Spirit would come to stay with us upon repentance, recognition and confessing that we are sinners, and asking Him to come into our lives believing that He's coming back for his church, God's Holy Spirit abiding with David throughout his reign was the secret of his greatness.

Jewish historians portray David as having several harems without documentation of numbers. Biblical history by contrast has David with two dozen or less wives also without specific numbers. Concubine is defined as a secondary wife. So we have no accurate account of David's wives. When you consider David's popularity since his conquest of Goliath (1 Samuel 18:16), "But all Judah and Israel loved David...," I think it reflects constraint on the part of David when he could have easily had the 700 wives and 300 concubines his son Solomon had (1 Kings 11:3). With so many wives it's a no-brainer as to his testosterone level. We visit the episode of his first encounter with Bathsheba. 2 Samuel 11:2: "And it came to pass at eventide that David arose from his bed, and walked upon the roof of the King's house. And from the roof he saw a woman washing herself, and the woman was very beautiful to look upon." What did he see? It's obvious she would not be a petite woman if he could see her. If she's naked her face would not be the first physical feature to be observed. I'm sure her physiognomy was part of the "beautiful" to look at analysis. But we cannot dismiss her physical composition. She was probably voluptuous, this was poetry to look at. And we find him doing a normal thing, salivating. The lust of the eyes and the lust of the flesh take charge (1 John 2:16). We have to keep in mind he had many wives but there's something "different," distinct, contrasting from anything he had experienced to date, an overwhelming novelty. This was a tantalizing obsession that would not let go. After all, he was the King, he was entitled to the best of everything but there was nothing in his kingdom as fine as what he's observing. At work here is a war between the primal animal instincts of the body, working in concert with the "emotions" of the Soul against the Spirit/Godconciousness. This struggle cannot be minimized. This diabolical duo wins a temporary victory (see Chapter II). Three of God's 10 Commandments, written by the hand of Moses, are violated. And yes, there were consequences.

I recall in my private practice two female counselees who had been a part of the nightlife and were seeking advice on reform based on offers of marriage. Both had shared with me a colloquialism: "Variety is the spice of life." Their further explanation was that they found men in this traffic were usually seeking something "different" as a turn-on. Variety. This is consistent with the studies that men who had affairs had usually fantasized something different.

David's initial lust ends with obsessive love for this woman Bathsheba was of African descent, a Black woman. This, in my opinion was the "different" the distinction that set her apart from all the wives and concubines. The "different" would include all of her physical features. Although we are not told directly that Bathsheba is a Hamite, we can actually trace her heritage through her grandfather Ahithophel (David's African counselor). In 2 Samuel 11:3 we are told that Bathsheba's father is Eliam, but it isn't until 2 Samuel 23 that we find out that Bathsheba's grandfather is a Gilonite. There is still some debate of her lineage the question of her race to some is still an open one. I believe that the voluptuous contrast of this woman was so profound that its distinction erupted from ethnic characteristics.

I'm remembering during my college years I worked for a distinguished laboratory. My boss was a proud self-proclaimed redneck. This was 1963, before the passing of the civil rights bill. I was their first African-American on board. Hewey grew up in the Deep South all of his life and didn't interact with Blacks until military service. He was a major in the Air Force during WWII. In conversation he shared with me the culture shock he experienced in seeing in his words "these Black buxsomed women of size and shape, I have never seen anything like this before." This exchange, of course, adds to my conviction. The reasons I believe that there was no outcry from the populous at that time because of her race was twofold. One her extraordinary beauty and two the consequences of public declared racism. Just 400 years earlier, their greatest prophet Moses had married an African, i.e. an Ethiopian woman. Moses' brother and sister complained and sneered about this alliance. God was so upset with this in-your-face racism that He put the worst disease, leprosy, on Miriam for her actions (Numbers 12). After her repentance she was healed. All Israel witnessed this and would never forget. There were no Bibles, no libraries, or bookstores to communicate this episode. The printing press was many hundreds of years away, this history was passed down through "Oral Tradition." Each generation would hear this story for 400 years. They never forgot. What intrigues me most about David and Bathsheba is that we find no more nuptial ties or marriages after her. The last becomes the first. No other wife bears as many children for him after their marriage. She gives him four sons, beginning with Solomon. We will never know how many sons and daughters David had with wives and concubines but his level of testosterone for this giant among men was unquestionable.

Interracial marriage is almost as old as time. Fast forward to the 21st century. With all the international hate, tragedy, pain and turmoil, the world stood still for the enchanting euphoria we experienced in watching the wedding of handsome Prince Harry and his beautiful Black bride Meghan. Witnessing the eye contact between this duo brought us the heartwarming confirmation of true love. Here, this powerful testament of true love was happening in this stellar fairytale pageantry, White and Black joined together under the umbrella of holy matrimony. Coming to the defense of her beloved grandson's ethnic choice, Queen Elizabeth shocked her court and the world in revealing the centuries-old secret that the royal family had African blood in its lineage. True love won the day. It worked for Moses, King David and why not them?

On the other side of the testosterone spectrum we have Boaz. Boaz is the great-grandfather of David. Boaz was certainly not a David. Boaz becomes the biological great, great, great, great-grandfather of Jesus. Boaz by history would be considered average to low testosterone level. He was happy to have just one wife, Ruth. The study of Boaz suggests a much older man marrying this younger beautiful widow. They have one son, Obed, the grandfather of David.

There's no widely accepted measure of what is a healthy level of sex desire, according to the American Medical Association. Some people want to have sex every day, or more than once a day, others once a year or not at all. However, a person who lacks a desire for sexual activity for some period of time may be experiencing a hypoactive sexual desire disorder or may be asexual. Asexual desire disorder is more common in women than men, and women tend to express less frequent and less intense sexual desires than men.

As a couple you have months and years to explore and discover what will work for you. This is one of the great adventures of marriage. If there are medical challenges always get two or three opinions. I'm reminded of a personal situation I had a few years ago. I have an extra molar in my upper jaw that is laying horizontally. I had gone to three older dentists who gave me the same diagnosis. They had to break my jaw to solve the problem.

Finally, I said to myself, why not consult with a younger dentist/ What did I have to lose? Sure enough he said, "Old school was to break the jaw to remove it, let me ask you, is it bothering you?" to which I replied no. He responded, "Then I would leave it alone." What a relief.

The most important part of this writing in my opinion is the Epilogue. Because God has created us as eternal entities it behooves us to be prepared for our final destination after this life. In this life is our duty as Christians to "let our lights so shine..." in our marriages because the world is watching and our marriage is supposed to be a reflection of God's relationship to His church.

Appendix 1

Isaiah 43:11: "I, even I am the Lord, and beside me there is no savior." John 14:6: "Jesus saith unto him, I am the way, the truth, and the life; no man cometh unto the Father, but by Me." Acts 4:12: "Neither is their salvation in any other; there is no other name under heaven given among men, whereby we must be saved."

A SINNER'S PRAYER

> Dear God, I acknowledge that I am a sinner. I now repent of all the sins that I have committed against God and man. I want you, Lord Jesus, to come into my life and save me. I acknowledge that you, Lord Jesus, are the son of God, and that you died for my sins and rose again on the third day and now sit at the right hand of God our Father. I accept you as my Lord and savior by faith. Now believe by faith that God has saved you. Romans 10:9: "If thou shalt confess with thy mouth the Lord Jesus, and shall believe in thine heart that God has raised Him from the dead, thou shalt be saved."

Rejection from God is not possible. God guarantees your acceptance into His family. "...Him that cometh to me I will in nowise cast out" (John 6:37). Your life will never be the same. You now have a creator that will be with you from every mountaintop to valley in your life's journey; who will never leave you or forsake you. "...I am with you always, even unto the end of the age" (Matthew 28:20). You can look forward to over one thousand promises that culminate with Psalms 34:19: "Many are the afflictions of the righteous; but the Lord delivereth him out of them all."

Find a gospel preaching/teaching church and seek fellowship and baptism. There are over one million pastors and evangelists in the United States alone. I encourage you to follow the TV or internet five of my favorites (they can be accessed by most countries): Charles Stanley, Jentezen Franklin, T.D. Jakes, Rabbi Kurt Schneider and The 700 Club. Catch us on the web and YouTube (*www.aspecialfreegift.com*).

Appendix 2
SAVED FROM

Our Sins: Matthew 1:21: "And she shall bring forth a son and thou shalt call his name Jesus, for he shall save his people from their sins."

This Present Evil World: Galatians 1:4: "Who gave himself for our sins that he might deliver us from our present evil world according to the will of God and our Father."

Satan Power of Darkness: Colossians 1:13: "Who hath delivered us from the power of darkness...." Acts 26:18: "To open their eyes, and to turn them from darkness to light, and from the power of Satan unto God."

Hell/The Lake of Fire: Revelation 20:12-15: "And I saw the dead, small and great, stand before God and the books were open...and whosoever was not found in the book of life was cast into the lake of fire." Luke 10:20:" "... Rejoice because your names are written in heaven (Jesus speaking)."

Appendix 3
Enemies of the Christian

The World

1 John 2:15, 16: *"Love not the world. Neither the things that are in the world. If any man love the world, the love of the Father is not in him. For all that is in the world, the lust of the flesh and the lust of the eyes, and the pride of life, is not of the Father, but is of the world."*

The Flesh

Romans7:17, "...But sin that dwelleth in me." Romans 7:18: *"For I know that in me (that is in my flesh) dwelleth no good thing; read verses 19-25.*

The Devil

1 Peter 5:8: *"Be sober, be vigilant, because your adversary, the devil, like a roaring lion walketh about, seeking whom he may devour."* II Tim 2:26 *"And that they may recover themselves out of the snare of the devil, who are taken captive by him at his will. (KJV)* He was created as the highest arch angel and through pride, rebelled

against God and was thrown out of heaven. He took 1/3 of the angelic host with him. That's hundreds of thousands of dark entities; each having the power to enable demons & evil spirits. All with power to control both mind and body of humans & animals. Young, old, rich, poor, Black, White, Etc. No non-born again Believer is exempt!!! The solution, the cure, the only antidote is the presence of God's Holy Spirit in your spirit domain. This happens only by your invitation—CHOICE. The truly born again believer cannot be demon possessed.

Autobiography (PARTIAL)

I was born in the end of WWII. My mother told me I was her only physical comfort there on the island of Jamaica as she worried during this wartime era and waited for her soldier husband to come home to her. At 9 months old I accompanied her to NYC, where citizenship was granted based on my father's veteran status. I grew up in Brooklyn and attended Boys High. I got saved at the age of 9 on my mother's birthday, 2/14/54, she was a Valentine's Day baby and married at the young age of 15. They lived together for 49 years when she passed. Being saved at that young age was the most exciting thing that had ever happened to me at that time. Even more impressive than becoming a Cub Scout at 8 years old. This took place in Sunday school at Good Tidings Gospel Hall, Brooklyn, NY. This was the largest Brethren church in NYC. The Brethren was a denomination that emphasized in "The Word." They were strictly biblical literalists, interpreting the Bible literally. As a result of this discipline, I became an avid Bible reader from age 9. Unfortunately, from 10 to 14 years old there were no youth groups or fellowships for young people. You were treated as an adult as far as spiritual growth. JHS became my teacher from age 11. The growing interest in girls and youth hormones spiraling out of control told another story. At the age of 14, now in my 1st year of high school I discovered the power of music. Quite by accident I put together a sensational rock-'n-roll group. Why sensational? A talent scout from END Recording Co. came to hear our 4th rehearsal, after listening, wanted to sign us. I refused the offer because he wanted us to get rid of our bassist who was tone deaf and just happened to be my best friend. This would've meant surrendering him to the gang-ridden streets in the projects he lived in. In my 4 years with the group we never had another offer like that again. Our 1st gig was at Girls High School. Over 300 girls screaming and swooning to our sound. This was both shocking and electrifying. The 4 years that followed exposed us to music stars, fame, partying and of course, the opposite sex. It was a norm to date 20-30 females at a time. I lived in a Jewish neighborhood, considered as middle class. I got caught up with the plastic fame for 3 years. I had fallen away from my faith and at the same time was now growing tired of this partying scene. One night during this time, I fell under conviction in my room and began weeping. I asked God to forgive me of all the partying and sins I had committed. As I got up from praying I reached out to lay hold on my Bible which hadn't been touched for over 4 years, and opened to a book I had never read. Malachi 3:7: "...Return unto me, and I will return unto you, saith the Lord of hosts...." I can't tell you the joy I experienced in reading this. A divine confirmation that God had heard my prayer and was welcoming me home. Wow!!!

It was around this time a young, powerful, dynamic evangelist had moved into the neighborhood, just two doors down from me.

There could be no question about the special anointing over his life. Tom Skinner was *New York Times* front-page news at the age of 22. I had heard him years earlier at a Harlem Crusade. He had now come from Harlem to live next door to me in Brooklyn. As I look back now, I realized that this was no coincidence on God's calendar. As for Tom, after writing his first book, *Black and Free*, he was no longer welcomed in most Black Baptist circles. He had joined the Brethren church where I fellowshipped from a child. Dr. Arthur Garnes had become one of his friends and mentors. It was shortly after my midnight conviction, I was invited by Tom to a revival meeting he was having at the Hopkinson Avenue Brethren Church in Brooklyn. They had welcomed him there and gave him an office free of charge to begin his worldwide ministry. At the close of that meeting I had accepted his invitation to rededicate my life to Jesus Christ and look forward to a new chapter in my life. As the only candidate that came forward that night (it was a small gathering) I received a lot of attention from Tom and the elders—the Noel brothers and their sister. This was to begin a unique bond between Tom and myself from these teenage years. I can tell you that some of his counseling in those years were really rough. Both Tom and Dr. Arthur Garnes would be integral in my spiritual development in the years that followed. But now I had a big problem. I felt compelled to leave the group I had started. I had been a father figure to some of these young men for 4 years. They were outraged. I prayed in earnest and asked God to help me in this dilemma. God answered my prayer within 3 weeks.

I just happened to be walking through one of the wards at the Jewish Chronic Disease Hospital in Brooklyn where I worked (while attending college part time) and heard this awesome voice, the voice belonged to Al Moore, who was the lead singer for "THE PARAGONS." When I explain my situation, he was very interested. After he came and met them, and sang 2 numbers with our background it was like a marriage of the ages to me. I still have that recording. In my vanity, I reveled in the fact that our harmony was far superior to this older and seasoned famous group. They went on as a group for a number of years. With today's technology you can hear Al. Just go to YouTube and put either "Al Moore/Blue Velvet" or "The Paragons/Blue Velvet." I had spent a number of teenage years visiting the home of Dr. Arthur Garnes and had learned so much from him. If you're wondering why so many visits, I had met his oldest daughter at a high school track meet. On one encounter I had asked him had he ever thought about writing a book and what might its subject be. He made it clear that he had no intention of such and would rather have his life read as a book. In those days, he was an accomplished pianist. I enjoyed being a spectator on several occasions. My musical taste began transitioning from doo-wop to classical. Doc's favorite piano concerto was Mozart's 21s, mine was Mozart's 22nd, particularly the 1st and 3rd movement. It reminded me of my life. I was always struck by his massive library which consisted of both medical and theological books. I didn't find out till many years later that Arthur Garnes, M.D., was famous for being the first Black plastic surgeon in the world. Both he and Brother Wilks from Grace Brethren Church in Harlem, NY, were the humblest people I had ever known. One rich and one poor. I tried throughout my life to pattern their example. So many decades had passed since I had seen him. I visited him in Maryland, when I found out that he was still alive at age 97. He died at age 99. When I recently Googled him, true to form, he never wrote that book. Somehow I do recall one of his favorite scriptures was John 3:30: "He must increase and I must decrease."

While attending college part time at age 20 there were a lot of rumors circulating that a major war was imminent. I feared I wouldn't be married if that happened. So I rushed into a marriage with a girl I had fallen in love with and enjoyed a beautiful wedding in Jamaica and honeymoon in Montego Bay. 2 months later I was drafted into the United States Army. By dropping out of college to get married, my name was picked up by the draft board. You can't imagine how furious I was as a newlywed. The 23rd Psalm would become a personal reality: "Yea though I walk through the valley of the shadow of death...." Not knowing when you might be called to the front line could be anxiety provoking if you had little faith. I lost 58,000 friends and comrades in that war. It would take a book to express these mostly agonizing 24 months that did include some inspiration highs. I would have called that book "Clouds Over Bragg." One of those highs was a developmental relationship I had experienced with the Ku Klux Klan. Suffice it to say, God was with me through my tour of duty, I had the distinction of leaving the Army as being the only man in the history of the United States Army to make Sargent "SP5" E5 in less than 4 months. Through God's grace favor and mercy. This would typically take 2-3 years, I would put this on every re sume which always ignited a conversation. Tom had witnessed my metamorphosis from the young teenage counselee to the up-and-coming young preacher he worked with after my 2-year service commitment in the U.S. Army. When I came home from the Army, I was on fire to preach the Gospel. I had met Ralph Bell while in service. He was the 2nd Black associate of the Billy Graham association. Second to Howard Jones, who I would meet 3 years later at a Christian Black leadership meeting.

As a chaplain assistant, I had the opportunity of spending hours of quality time with Brother Bell which contributed to my spiritual ambitions in the years ahead. So, I wasn't surprised when I received an invitation to join the Billy Graham evangelical team as a trainee years later.

Soul/Dimension

Somehow my love for music accompanied my fervor for preaching the Gospel. I realized a good sound would always attract people. Why not attract them to the message of the cross?? With this inspiration I started the first Gospel rock group in NYC, conceptualizing it as concert crusades. Our target was the inner city, especially projects and college campuses in the tristate area. We could put on our resume the Apollo Theatre and the most memorable John Hancock Hall—the Carnegie Hall of Boston, Massachusetts, where we rocked that place to a standing-only audience. Soul Dimension's one goal was to win souls for Christ. Our sound easily rivaled today's *American Idol.* When we entered the project complexes, we never knew if we would be met by hundreds or thousands we would entertain, followed by the message and an invitation to accept Jesus. Hundreds listened from their sometimes 20-story windows. Our sound system would carry for 2 city blocks. We did, however, falter in our follow-up, lacking the man power. I can only hope in that 7-year era, 1969-1976, that some seeds fell on good ground. If I had a wish list, it would be the ability to turbocharge the microcosm of soul dimension's activities into this 21st century, covering Europe and Asia. Now in the late 60s into the 70s marked a turning point in the evangelical community as it faced civil rights history. I had recalled in the early 60s during my early college years being awestruck by one William F. Buckley, a white intellectual prodigy who had no equal. His superb eloquence and articulation of speech was only exceeded by his arrogance. Here on a PBS special is where I experienced Malcolm X for the first time. I could not believe what I was experiencing. Malcolm chewed him up, spit him out and destroyed him to the amazement of the millions of viewers watching. This tape seemed to have mysteriously disappeared from YouTube's archives. Shortly after that PBS produced another amazing interview called "Open Mind (6 12-63)" with Dr. Wyatt T. Walker, James Farmer and Malcolm X. These are today available on YouTube. It was 30 years later I would meet Wyatt at the President's club at Newark Airport. When I mentioned the Malcolm X interview as how I recognized him from it, it sparked a friendship that flourished over the next 15 years. Wyatt was responsible for introducing me to a number of notable people in his circle like Reverend Dr. Blackshear, president of the minister's conference, who engaged me to address his constituency upon introduction. We met on several occasions at the club during those years. In all our conversations I never knew that he was the chief of staff to Martin Luther King Jr. until I Googled him years later. Wyatt was the classiest Black preacher I had ever known, standing shoulder to shoulder with my idol George William Webber (President of New York Theological Seminary, Emeritus), the classiest White preacher I had ever known. I was both amazed and flattered that Bill and two other of my professors at seminary commented that I reminded them of one of their famous alumni, Pat Robertson.

I look forward to the day where we stand in the presence of God and I hear Him say to Bill Webber, "Well done, my good and faithful servant." You would have to be in Bill's presence for just 5 minutes to experience the love an electrifying inspiration he exuded. When I think of the countless thousands of students and people he touched, there are no adjectives to describe his greatness. My interview with Bill was my first academic contact with New York Theological Seminary, where I shared my vision of CDS with him. I will always remember him as a caring friend. One of the greatest experiences I had at NYTS came on graduation day. There at the ceremony with several hundred people I see a 6'5" blonde-hair, blue-eyed giant, the chaplain I served 15 years earlier in the 82nd airborne. In amazement I called to him "Chaplain Durham, 82nd airborne." He rushes to me and picks me up in my graduation gown in front of my parents, friends, and attendees, what a reunion.

The question of equality, civil rights and evangelism was center stage in the 60s and 70s era. Billy Graham had grappled with this problem and engaged Howard Jones, a Black preacher, to facilitate transitions that would allow for integrated crusade audiences. Billy had also tried to work covertly in helping Martin Luther King in his quest. Overall, most white evangelicals took the position of 2 Timothy 2:4: "No man that warreth entangeleth himself with the affairs of this life, that he may please Him who hath chosen him to be a soldier." Hands-off politics, this would leave the burden of civil rights issues on people like Tom Skinner to address the problem. Urbana 1970 gave him that opportunity. I was thrilled to be one of the handful of Blacks to go and support him there in Illinois among the 15,000 attending this intervarsity extravaganza. During that week of meetings and workshops, Tom made it clear that he would take up arms if necessary to defend his family as a constitutional right and God-given responsibility. This did cost him the financial support of many white evangelicals at that time. They saw him as militant by not maintaining the "turn the other cheek" status quo. Urbana was a moment in history that will never be forgotten (you can Google Urbana 1970 and hear the message).

Many years had passed and now I found myself reaching out to Tom to be a commentator on an infomercial I was directing for CDS. I flew down to Maryland, where he had bought a farm in hopes of fulfilling one of his dreams to centralize his ministry. It was amazing to me to see this former gang leader on his hands and knees planting in his fields as I drove up. It was his goal at that time to consolidate his many ministry obligations to a number of professional sport teams. He wanted to build a track, pool, etc., to accommodate them versus all the indigenous travel he endured in his status quo. In conversation, I asked, "Tom, as you look back, is there anything you would have done differently in your ministry?" He paused, then responded, "I would have devoted more time to prayer." As I was preparing to leave he offered me an invitation to come to his 50th Birthday celebration. I explained why that wouldn't be possible because of the deadlines I was facing. The infomercial ran in New York for 1 year. This was the last time I would see my friend. Tom passed away 2 years later and I wasn't aware of this for at least a year. There are no words to describe such a loss to the world. Tom had frequented 26 countries with the Gospel and was viewed by a consensus of pastors to be one of the greatest evangelists in the 20th century. I'm so glad that modern technology makes him available to our younger generation. I close this CDS chapter of my life by sharing the greatest surprise I'd ever witnessed in my personal life. At one of our socials at CDS, a woman walks up to me and says, "Wes, my father wants to help you, can you come to Washington this February—at an affair we're having?" I responded I would not be able but maybe another time (hoping she would forget). The following year she remembered, and I obliged her. I was to meet a man I had never heard of.

She introduced me to her dad, Dr. Ben Armstrong, president of the NRB (a worldwide organization). He invited me to their home in Madison, NJ, for lunch. He walks me through their hallway and tells me, "I'm responsible for putting the last 6 Republican Presidents in office. Do you know who Billy Graham is?" "Of course," my reply. "Do you know who Jerry Fallwell is?" My reply, "Absolutely." "Well, they report to me." He's at the same time pointing out pictures on the wall of him with all the Presidents since Eisenhower. I'm bewildered and asking myself, "Who is this man?" Ben then walks me back to the kitchen table where his wife is sitting and says, "Wes, we've been watching you, and have been very impressed. President Bush (the 1st Bush was in office at that time) is in need of a cabinet member and I want you to accept this nomination, it would be a done deal." Can you imagine my shock??? Reader, pause for 3 minutes and put yourself in my shoes. How would you respond? What would you be thinking?? I was working on building a national sales force for CDS at the time. Even being surrounded by so many smart people, I realized that this was something only I could do. And this would require 12/7 time capsule to do it. This was all pre-internet.

I was emphatic about my goal and the commitment it would take to accomplish it in my conversation with Ben. The conversation went on for about 20 minutes. I'm sure they were equally surprised at my reluctance. Finally, Ben says, "Do you know who Eldridge Cleaver is?" "Why, sure, Ben." He responds, "I'm responsible for bringing him back to America." Eldridge Cleaver was one of the founders of the Black Panther party. J. Edgar Hoover had put a hit out on all of its leadership in the 60s. Reading between the lines, I think Ben was saying no matter what kind of trouble you may have been in, we can cover that. I thanked him again and again and begged him to understand the gravity of what I was trying to do. This experience so overwhelmed me I suppressed it in my subconscious and told no one. Almost 5 years later I woke up one morning and said to myself on reflection, "Wow, I never told my sons about this episode." This was going to be the 1st time I'd told anyone. I would go on to continue the ministry for another 14 years. During this quarter-of-a-century commitment—1980-2004—I witnessed tens of thousands of relationships with hundreds of marriages to the glory of God. I never took a salary. It was my contribution to the Christian Singles Community.

EPILOGUE

Hitherto our focus has been on the duo. Here in the conclusion of matters, I am compelled to draw your attention to you. In my opinion, the most terrifying verses of scripture in the Bible are found in Matthew 7:21-23: "Not everyone that saith unto me Lord, Lord shall enter into the kingdom of heaven, but he that doeth the will of my Father who is in heaven. Many will say to me in that day, Lord, Lord have we not prophesied in thy name and in thy name cast out demons?... And then will I profess unto them, I never knew you, depart from me ye that work iniquity." English Standard Version (ESV) 2 Corinthians 13:5: "Examine yourselves to see if you are in the faith. Test yourselves. Or do you not realize this about yourselves, that Jesus Christ is in you?—Unless indeed you fail to meet the test!" I can't think of any word more loosely used in the English language than the word "Christian." The older I get the more amazed I become. The word Christian is defined "Christlike," the average person would respond when asked that they consider themselves Christian. However, stay in a conversation for 15-20 minutes and you probably end up with a different conclusion. And if the opportunity of days or weeks are available with that person, behavior usually tells a different story. This was a problem before the church was founded. Here Jesus had thousands who followed him and were converted in their hearts from his powerful message. But knowing man, he recognized that there would be those who simply gave lip service. That's why he would say, "...Why call ye me, Lord, Lord and do not the things which I say?" (Luke 6:46). Or "...My mother and my brethren are these who hear the word of God, and do it" (Luke 8:21). True Christianity is a lifestyle that demands your inner spirit to be fed daily. Especially with the onslaught of our three enemies (the world, the flesh, and the devil—see Appendix 3), harassing us on a daily basis. Is even in responsible positions in the church, but they have only a "head"—or intellectual—acceptance of the Lord Jesus Christ. Tragically enough, even teachers, preachers, and religious workers are not exempt from the possibility of the chilling indictment above.

The distance between the head and the heart is 18 inches. Unfortunately, a "head" knowledge of Jesus Christ—fully knowing and giving mental assent to the plan of salvation...without also a "heart" acceptance that brings the personal relationship that the Bible demands—avails nothing to anyone. Listen to Paul's heart cry concerning Israel as he spoke under the HOLY SPIRIT: "For I bare them record that they have a zeal of God, but not according to knowledge." He was speaking about misdirected efforts energies expended in the strength of the flesh but not under the direction of the HOLY SPIRIT. The lack of power today in many of our churches, as well as the lack of power today in the lives of many professing Christians, can be laid directly to this.

It is only as we see ourselves in the mirror of God's word as without excuse and without hope utterly lost and undone that the truth of the Scriptures convicts for the Bible clearly reveals that this is how God sees us. Then when the wonder truth of the Gospel brings us to the recognition of our own sinfulness, and in true repentance we cry out to God asking forgiveness and help, asking Him to come into our hearts, not our heads, we experience the new birth.

Jesus Christ said, "I am the way, the truth, and the life; no man cometh unto the Father but by Me." The Bible also tells us that "He that hath the son has eternal life, and he that hath not the son of God has not life." Also, the Bible promises, "If thou shalt confess with thy mouth the Lord Jesus, and shall believe in thine heart that God raised him from the dead, thou shalt be saved. But with the heart man believeth unto righteousness; and with the mouth confession is made unto salvation." Christ wants your heart, not just your head, because "The Lord seeth not as man seeth; for man looketh on the outward appearance but the Lord looketh on the heart." It is vitally important that you make sure it is not just head knowledge and mental assreaent you have given to Jesus Christ. He needs your complete trust so that you can be truly born again. "18 inches can mean eternity with Christ or an eternity without Christ. Are you sure of your personal relationship to him?"

Not sure? See Appendix 1.

2 Tim. 2:26: "And that they may recover themselves out of the snares of the devil, who are taken captive by him at his will." In my opinion, this is the scariest fact of life in human existence. Imagine an invisible entity that could invade your mind and body at will: rich or poor; black white yellow or brown; tall or short; fine or ugly; good or bad. If there was any reason I would want

to get saved it would be for this divine protection I would have from this enemy (see Append. number 3). Satan's power was nailed to Jesus' cross, life's only defense. Hundreds of millions of people are confronted each day with this reality. One of the Devil's greatest strategies is to convince the world that he does not exist. He has been successful in doing this. The question is elementary. Do you believe God, who says he does exist? Or do you believe him?

The story is told that Satan had a big conference and invited all of his top generals to this meeting. His topic was how could he get more candidates/people in to HELL. Dozens of ideas came to the floor. Finally, one top general stood up and said, "Just tell them they have time." They all responded with glee. This was the answer. Procrastination is one of our greatest enemies. Do any of us know when the death angel will knock on our door??? We know not the day nor the hour. An average of 168,000 died today, 168,000 will die tomorrow and the next day and on and on how many of them knew they were leaving this earth??? They were young and old; rich and poor; black and white, death does not discriminate. Eternity is real and forever. You have it in your power to choose your final destination!!! Tomorrow is not promised to you.

> Friend,
>
> We are now in 2021 facing the most perilous time in human existence. We are actually in the last days. The end of time for the Church, not the world. No, we don't know the day or the hour, that's a given. "But of that day and hour knoweth no man, no, not the angels of heaven, but my

Father only (Matt. 24:36)." But we do have the sense of the season based on prophesy. There is controversy among Bible scholars in the interpretation of the sequence of events in these last days such as: ' pre-trib' & 'post-trib.' Example, pre-trib thinking- Christians will be raptured (taken up to be with the Lord) before the great tribulation. Or, post-trib thinking – Christians will go through the great tribulation and then be raptured. This is just one of several points of contention among Bible scholars. However, the consensus is that there is pin point accuracy to date to confirm prophetic occurrences that we are in fact in the last days. It behooves every true Christian in this time and era to seek Bible studies on prophesy.

Hal Lindsey in June 2020 made a statement in humor, which I consider profound. He's a pre-triber. He said, "there will be millions of professing Christians who straddled the fence and saw their real Christians friends and family taken and then realize they were left behind. They are the ones who will then believe and work feverishly to do good and evangelize. However, because of the times they will be tortured and brutally murdered etc. Smiling, he concluded, wouldn't it make sense to join God's family now and avoid all that suffering?"

Another pre-tribber is Irvin Baxter (End Time Ministries), whose committed to prophesy in following the events of Israel & the Palestinians. His conclusion is that a peace deal between the 2 countries is imminent. I was impressed after viewing the peace proposal and the United States involvement. This was a work of genius. J. Kushner should receive international recognition. Sanctions for both sides are cited for anticipated violations. Irvin's interpretation is that according to prophesy, the day the agreement is signed marks the beginning of the seven year tribulation. And that half way into the 7 years, both sides renege and war breaks out in the region. Armageddon starts at the close of the 7 year tribulation. Pretribbers believe that the Church will be raptured before Armageddon. It behooves us to study both pre & post views.

I spent 30 years studying testimonies of Christians who had died and came back to life miraculously. They all told the same story of heaven and hell. Twenty plus years ago (circa) Mary K. Baxter wrote "A Divine Revelation of Hell." She took this to another level. It did corroborate what I had learned from the other testimonies. In summary, Jesus takes her for 30 consecutive nights into different parts of hell. What intrigued me most was that there was a special part of hell reserved for church folks. Hell is real. God is real. The enemy is real.

OUR BLESSED ASSURANCE

"...And the dead in Christ shall rise first, then we who are alive and remain shall be caught up together with them in the clouds, to meet the Lord in the air; and so shall we ever be with the Lord. Wherefore, comfort one another with these words"

(1 Thessalonians 4:16, 17).

PHOTO GALLERY

My Parents Ralph and Gwendolyn Mullings

Kids on Block

Singing Group

Basic Training

Wes with Rev. Bell

Rev. Bell and Chaplain Durham

Wes and Rich in Uniform

Sgt Wes

Soul Dimension

1969 - 1976
SOUL DIMENSION
DATE:

1980 - 2004
CHRISTIAN DATING SERVICE INT'L
NON-DENOMINATIONAL
CHRISTIAN DATING SERVICE INT'L
"Our Story"

Our Story . . .

After hundreds of hours of phone conversations and thousands of letters received since the inception of this Ministry, we at C D S have had to take a closer look at the problems that face approximately 25 million Christian Singles across the nation; not to mention the World at large. Singles are a culture unto themselves, bearing the brunt of problems that are co-related to their status.

They ask such questions as: Will I ever find someone? Are there any good men/women left? Am I inadequate in relationships? What are my chances of finding a relationship in my _________ category? Will my emotional scars continue to hinder other relationships? Where can I meet Christians who are also single??? A significant number of our applicants have confided in us that they left the Church because of the Social dryness. Though we at CDS will agree that this *is not* a primary Spiritual concern, we must recognize the variation of Spiritual levels on an individual basis.

Christian singles by the thousands have flocked to the harbors of the World to escape loneliness. So many of these have been caught in the trap of being "Unequally yoked (11 Cor. 6:14);" many which have ended in tragedy. Our interviewing process has also revealed that many singles feel somewhat alienated within the Church Institution because of what they experience as predominantly family oriented activities.

It is our experience that most members are interested in marriage to a Christian mate; however, the remainder are interested only in Social fellowship. C D S is successfully fulfilling both needs nation-wide and World-wide. One of our major concerns is matching people in *like* as well as *similar* Faiths to help insure compatibility. the concept of intermediating social relationships is far from a new one, the Biblical accounts of Jacob, Ruth, and Samson are but a few examles. Within the Body of Christ, C D S functions as a 'gift of helps (1 Cor. 12:28),' a ministry to ". . . bind up the broken-hearted. . . . (Is. 61:1)."

All of our lines of communication and servicing are monitored through our International base of operation at "Miracle Mansion," Orange, New Jersey. Here, we literally match people WITHIN their State and Tri-State areas, whether it be in Los Angles, California or Athens, Greece; Brooklyn, New York or the Republic of China. Loneliness holds no regard for denominational lines whether one is Lutheran, Baptist, Presbyterian, Catholic or otherwise, being a "peculiar people" (1 Pe. 2:9) called out to be separate has compounded a problem that we at C D S cannot eliminate but continue to help alleviate. We admonish our members that we *are not* the answer to founding personal relationships, merely a vehicle, not to look to us to consumate such; but to look to God to work *through* us.

As a Pastor or Religious leader you can help us give the Christian Single Community a better sense of: Something to hope for, something to live for, and someone to love. Call or Write us for distribution of our literature at your Church or Organization.

Our Story

REV. STUART M. McKENZIE, President

Founder and Director of New Life Counseling Center, Vineland, NJ

Rev. McKenzie comes to the presidency of CDS Int'l with 15 yrs. of Pastoring experience among several Churches in the United Methodist Church. Among his contributions to Society are the 19 years he has given to the New Jersey Public School system. Rev. McKenzie holds several graduate degrees, 2 of which are from Princeton Theological Seminary — M.Div., Th.M. The testimony of his life is evidenced in his strong devotion to his wife and family. Nowadays "Stew" spends most of his time expanding his counciling Ministry and input in CDS Int'l's growing horizons.

"If you're like most Pastors, you don't have much time to deal with the Social needs of your parishioners. And yet these are real and viable needs, an area where hundreds of thousands in the Christian Community are hurting. For this reason thousands of Christians have frequented the harbors of the World to alleviate loneliness. Take a few minutes to read "Our Story;" it may add a dimension to your Ministry and Outreach."

The President

REV. VICTOR KEGLER, 1st V.P.
Assoc. Pastor, Salem Baptist Church, NJ

Former V.P. and Chaplain of Baptist Youth Fellowship; licensed to preach Feb. 13th, 1977. Attended Wiley College-Marshall, Texas. Presently an officer of the CHI ALPHA Christian Fellowship, Jersey City State College and Chairman of the Concerned Clergy of Jersey City.

DORI EVANS, Esq., 2nd V.P.
West Caldwell, New Jersey

Attended Bloomfield College 72-74; received her B.S. from Juniata College, PA in 1976. Received her J.D. from Franklin Pierce Law School, N.H. May 1980. Her expertise is in Corporate and Commercial Litigation as well as general practice. Dori is presently active in The Wall Street and Mid-town Business Prayer Group.

SID COHEN, C.P.A., Treasurer
Beaumont, Texas

Sid has been a practicing Certified Public Accountant for 19 years. He graduated from Northwestern University with a degree in Business Administration. Sid has served on the Board of Directors of several organizations in both Community and Church groups. His spiritual transition and active witness to being a Born Again Believer continues to spark admiration in his several business circles. Sid's experience and direction to our staff has not only been invaluable but a major factor in the expanding growth of CDS Int'l.

JOSEPH TURPIN, Secretary
Deacon, The Family Ministry Church
Orange, NJ

His under graduate work was done at Brookdale Community College and later Rutgers University, NJ. Joe has been an activist in a host of Social and Political organizations and served on many 'Boards' over the last 2 decades. Among his achievements: Fiscal Officer-Planned Parenthood of Middlesex County; General Mgr.-Ebony Enterprises Inc., Long Branch, NJ; Ass't Comptroller-Poverty Agency, Monmouth County.

Board of Directors

ADVISORY BOARD

FATHER GEORGE C. LUTZ, Pastor
Holy Spirit Roman Catholic Church
Orange, NJ

Ordained in 1962 at Immaculate Conception Seminary, Darlington, New Jersey. Graduate of Seton Hall University. Pastor Lutz has served as a teacher, councelor, administrator and other related services in both the Church and Community. His involvement in Community Action Groups and Ecumenical activities have been both dynamic and consistant. Organizations involved with include: C D S; Knights of Columbus; Lion's Club; American Legion; Civil Air Patrol; East Ward Two Association.

ROGER PUGSLEY, M.L.S.; Th.M.; M.Div.; M.A.
Research Analyst, CDS Int'l, Belleville, NJ

Roger is the son of the late world renowned Bible scholar Dr. James Wm. Pugsley. He is presently a librarian staff member at Northeastern Bible College. He serves on the staff of CDS Int'l as a Pastoral Councilor and our Biblical research Analyst. Among his alma mater's are: Princeton Theological Seminary; Westminister Theological Seminary; and Pratt Institute Graduate Library School. In addition to the critical analysis integral to our publications dept., Roger is Editor in Chief of our new International newspaper.

ANGELO GIAMMONA
Dir. of Religious Education - CDS Int'l
Hatfield, PA

Angelo's radical spiritual conversion eventually prompted him to leave a comfortable and secure teaching position of 15 yrs. with the Tom's River Board of Education to go into full time Ministry and Schooling. He has spent 7 years teaching, evangelizing and counciling with the American Board of Missions to the Jews. He is presently a Pastoral Councilor and Director of Religious education at CDS Int'l while finishing his Seminary training at Biblical Theological Seminary, Hatfield Pa.

Board of Advisors

WES MULLINGS, Coordinator
Christian Dating Service Int'l

Brother Wes received his B.A. at the State University of New York. His graduate degrees are in Pastoral Counciling and Psychology. His Post-graduate degree has come out of several Colleges of 'Hard knocks.' Former Ass't Chaplain 82 Airborne; Presently Assoc. Chaplain Bellevue Medical Center-NY; Director of The Family Ministry Church, Orange, NJ. Member of New York State, Marriage, Family and Child Counseling Assoc. and American Pastoral Psychological Assoc. Rev. Mullings was licensed and ordained in the Southern Baptist Church in 1970. He is the author of "On The Other Side Love . . . Sex . . . Marriage" (Vantage, 1970).

Wes, Coordinator

700 Club Film Crew

1980 – 2004

What Clerical Leaderships are Saying About

CHRISTIAN DATING SERVICE INT'L

(Serving Ages 18-80)

". . . in the multitude of Counselors there is safety" (Pr. 11:14)

Rev. Dr. Clay Evans
Fellowship Baptist Church - ILLINOIS

"In a day and time when so many innovations have enhanced the Ministry of the Church, Christian Dating Service Int'l is timely as one of those innovations that is glorifying God by building Christian Families across America. I personally endorse this Ministry."

Father George C. Lutz, Pastor
St. Peter Claver Catholic Church - NJ

"A historical episode in Ministry . . . I am proud to have had the privilege of observing the integrity of its operation first hand . . . an essential Ministry whose importance is further accentuated because of its Ecumenical outreach."

Dr. Timothy Birkett, President NYC
Protestant Conference of
Churches & Clergy

"My many years in counseling and ministry and particularly the Radio & T.V. Ministry God has called me to, has made me keenly sensitive to the needs of Christian singles in urban areas and what CDS is fulfilling for them. May this Ministry continue to grow in Grace."

Lt. Colonel John Durham, Chaplain
United States Army
Colorado Springs, CO

"Concurrent with our moving closer together with our speed of travel, intercontinental satellite capability etc . . . and our closer involvement with each other by means of on the spot world-wide t.v. reporting etc . . . a paradoxical problem has apparently arisen: that of loneliness, of isolation, it is expressed in the hunger for real contact with another human being. CDS is attempting to meet some of those needs. I whole-heartedly endorse this organization . . ."

Dr. Tom Skinner, Clergyman
World Renowned Evangelist

"In metropolitan areas it is increasingly difficult for single Christian people to find other single Christian people. Christian Dating Service is an idea whose time has come. I wholeheartedly support the concept."

Rev. Doug Cotton, Pastor
Assemblies of God, FL

"At last, someone with vision for a needed ministry, where the organized church has not wanted to get involved. I wholeheartedly support this ministry."

Clergy Endorsements

Dr. Benjamin Alicea, Chairman
Coalition of Hispanic Leadership, NY

"For years we have taught Christians in general and Christian youth in particular, to find Christian partners. Now we have a vehicle for facilitating this process in a creative and responsible manner. I wholeheartedly support the work and Ministry of C.D.S."

Dr. George W. Webber, Clergyman, Former President
N. Y. Theological Seminary

"In learning of the project from its director, I perceive that it is designed to meet a critical need of young people in our time; operating with sensitivity and intelligence. This should be a dynamic break-through in the Christian Community."

Dr. Keith A. Russell, Pastor
Baptist Church of the Redeemer - NY

"Christian Dating Service could be of great help to single Christians seeking to find each other. We wish this new Ministry well."

Rev. Glenn R. Hatfield, Pastor
First Baptist Peddie Memorial Church-NJ

"The idea behind Christian Dating Service makes sense. The service has produced 'success' for two fine Christian women from our Church — one young and one well along in maturity. Both are happily married ... and never would have found each other any other way. May God continue to bless this Ministry."

Rev. John Cadwell, Pastor
Church of the Nazarine - OH

"The world is full of lonely people. There is such a great need for Christian Singles to find companionship with other Christian Singles. I praise God that Christian Dating Service is meeting this need. I recommend, support and endorse this wonderful Ministry."

Rev. Daniel R. Schafer, Pastor
Assemblies of God, NJ

"I would like to express my appreciation for C.D.S. I have personally known two young people who have utilized its services with positive results in developing christian fellowship and later, marriage. Also, I have had the personal priviledge to speak at several of their socials and found it enriching. I would therefore not hesitate to recommend its' services to the Christian Community."

CHRISTIAN DATING SERVICE INT'L
BOX 678 SO. ORANGE, N.J. 07079

MARRIAGE TESTIMONIALS

Ecc.4:9 TWO ARE BETTER THAN ONE...

C D S has brought hundreds of couples together--NATIONWIDE, here are a few comments:

P.O. Box 678, So. Orange, New Jersey 07079
(www.christiandates.com)

MR. and MRS. GEORGE MOON
NORTHERN, PA

"For many reasons we both had reservations about using a dating service, even though this was a Christian one... Thank God for such an organization who brought us together . . . though so many miles apart (NJ-PA) . . . We owe our mariage and happiness to Christian Dating Service . . . May God continue to bless your Ministry."

MR. and MRS. ALLEN THURSTON
ASHLAND, VA

"No one wants to be alone and it is so hard to meet other Christians. We both prayed for christian mates but also *acted upon our Faith* (Faith w/o works is dead - Ja. 2:17) and joined your dating service . . . We will continue to recommend your Christian Dating Service to anyone concerned . . . We thank you again for bringing us together."

MR. and MRS. JACK THATCHER III
NEW YORK

"At first we were both not too keen about the idea of Christian Dating Service, but after much prayer the Lord directed us to you . . . indeed we are grateful as we both know that the Lord is indeed still working miracles through CDS (our friends tell us) . . . After our recent 16th wedding anniversary, we are still both very much in love . . . May God continue to bless CDS."

MR. and MRS. JOSEPH ST. CHARLES
SEATTLE, WASHINGTON

"The Lord has brought us together in the institution of marriage through Christian Dating Service Int'l. It started simply by corresponding and 1 year later it happened. Thank you again CDS for your help in bringing us together as you have done for so many couples across this country."

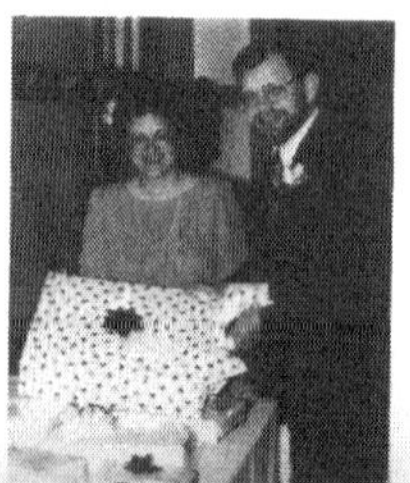

MR. and MRS. GEORGE MOON
NORTHERN, PA

"For many reasons we both had reservations about using a dating service, even though this was a Christian one... Thank God for such an organization who brought us together . . . though so many miles apart (NJ-PA) . . . We owe our mariage and happiness to Christian Dating Service . . . May God continue to bless your Ministry."

MR. and MRS. ALLEN THURSTON
ASHLAND, VA

"No one wants to be alone and it is so hard to meet other Christians. We both prayed for christian mates but also *acted upon our Faith* (Faith w/o works is dead - Ja. 2:17) and joined your dating service . . . We will continue to recommend your Christian Dating Service to anyone concerned . . . We thank you again for bringing us together."

MR. and MRS. JACK THATCHER III
NEW YORK

"At first we were both not too keen about the idea of Christian Dating Service, but after much prayer the Lord directed us to you . . . indeed we are grateful as we both know that the Lord is indeed still working miracles through CDS (our friends tell us) . . . After our recent 16th wedding anniversary, we are still both very much in love . . . May God continue to bless CDS."

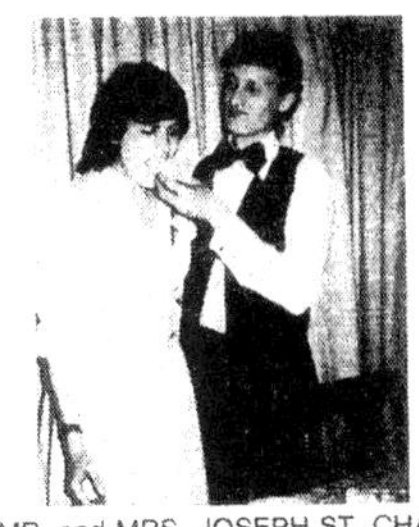

MR. and MRS. JOSEPH ST. CHARLES
SEATTLE, WASHINGTON

"The Lord has brought us together in the institution of marriage through Christian Dating Service Int'l. It started simply by corresponding and 1 year later it happened. Thank you again CDS for your help in bringing us together as you have done for so many couples across this country."

MR. and MRS. DONALD JOHANESEN
SALT LAKE CITY, UTAH

"We had romantic images of what we wanted that ignored our real needs . . . We came to know each other's heart and mind first . . . when we finally met it was 'love at first sight,' for our intellectual and emotional compatibility was already established . . . We thank you in Christ CDS, for bringing us together . . ."

MR. and MRS. MITCHELL MEDINA
NEW JERSEY

"After 17 years of marital bliss, we thank God over and over and over again for Christian Dating Service giving us to each other . . . What a blessing CDS turned out to be in our lives . . . Thank you Christian Dating Service for doing God's work faithfully."

Marriage Testimonials

Family Portrait